Illustrator:
Ken Tunell

Editors:
Barbara M. Wally, M.S.
Dona Herweck Rice

Editorial Project Manager:
Ina Massler Levin, M.A.

Editor in Chief:
Sharon Coan, M.S. Ed.

Art Director:
Elayne Roberts

Associate Designer:
Denise Bauer

Art Coordination Assistant
Cheri Macoubrie Wilson

Cover Artist:
Larry Bauer

Product Manager:
Phil Garcia

Imaging:
Ralph Olmedo, Jr.

Researcher:
Christine Johnson

Publishers:
Rachelle Cracchiolo, M.S. Ed.
Mary Dupuy Smith, M.S. Ed.

Author:

Mary Ellen Sterling, M.Ed.

Teacher Created Materials, Inc.
P.O. Box 1040
Huntington Beach, CA 92647
ISBN-1-57690-027-4

©1998 Teacher Created Materials, Inc.   Made in U.S.A.

Table of Contents

Table of Contents *(cont.)*

Introduction

The 20th Century is a series which examines the political, economic, social, cultural, scientific, and technological advances of the twentieth century, and introduces students to the individuals who made history in each decade.

The Fifties chronicles American life in the decade following World War II. Although the fighting had ended in Europe and the Pacific, new conflicts developed. When North Korean forces invaded South Korea in 1950, the United States led the United Nations-directed response. For three years the fighting continued and more than 33,000 American lives were lost. Meanwhile, a nuclear arms race added to the tension of the Cold War, in which the United States pledged its support to its former allies against the spread of the communist ideology of the Soviet Union.

The economy in the United States was prosperous. Many families moved to communities in the suburbs, and women resumed their traditional roles as mothers and homemakers. Television came into more and more homes during the fifties, changing the traditional lifestyle and the family structure.

By the middle of the decade, attention focused on civil rights, as African Americans voiced their feelings and called for an end to segregation. This battle against discrimination continued into the next decades. Discontent with the directions of society, the Beatniks adopted a rebellious lifestyle which included experimenting with drugs.

Knowledge and exploration grew immensely during this decade. Nuclear power plants began to create electricity, H-bombs were tested, and people lived in fear of a nuclear war. Some amazing scientific achievements focused attention elsewhere as the Russians launched the first artificial satellite and America began training astronauts for space flight. It was an exciting time to be alive.

This unit includes the following:

- ❑ a time line—a chronology of significant events of the decade
- ❑ planning guides—summaries and suggested activities for introducing the key issues and events of the decade
- ❑ personality profiles—brief biographies of important individuals of the decade
- ❑ a chronology of world events of the decade
- ❑ language experience ideas—suggestions for writing and vocabulary building
- ❑ group activities—assignments to foster cooperative learning
- ❑ topics for further research—suggestions for extending the unit
- ❑ literature connections—summaries of related books and suggested activities for expanding them
- ❑ curriculum connections—activities in math, art, language arts, social studies, and music
- ❑ computer applications— suggestions for selecting and using software to supplement this unit
- ❑ bibliography—suggestions for additional resources on the decade

To keep this valuable resource intact so that it can be used year after year, you may wish to punch holes in the pages and store them in a three-ring binder.

Time Line

	1950	1951
Politics and Economics	The Korean war begins when North Korea crosses the 38th parallel into South Korea on June 25. Senator Joseph McCarthy begins his hunt for communists.	The Rosenbergs are executed for spying against the United States. General MacArthur is relieved of his post by President Truman. The 22nd Amendment is passed; it limits the president to two terms. Congress passes the Mutual Security Act, authorizing almost $8 million in foreign aid.
Social and Cultural	The *Peanuts* comic strip is first published. Smokey the Bear becomes the symbol of forest fire safety. *The Adventures of Superman* starring George Reeves debuts on television. *Betty Crocker's Picture Cookbook* is published. The Henry J., a compact car, is introduced by Henry J. Kaiser. Minute Rice is introduced in supermarkets. The Nobel Peace Prize is awarded to United States diplomat Ralph J. Bunche, an African American. CBS television airs *Colorcast*, a commercial color transmission that stars Ed Sullivan and Arthur Godfrey.	Levittown, the first planned suburb, opens in New York. On October 5 *I Love Lucy* premieres on television.
Science and Technology	The first kidney transplant operation is performed.	The United States explodes an atomic bomb underground for the first time at Frenchman Flats, Nevada. UNIVAC I is the first electronic digital computer to be sold commercially. Electricity is first generated from atomic energy.

Time Line *(cont.)*

1952	1953	1954
Dwight D. Eisenhower is elected to the presidency. Puerto Rico becomes the first United States commonwealth.	Eisenhower is inaugurated as the 34th president; Richard Nixon is his vice-president. Earl Warren becomes Chief Justice of the Supreme Court. On July 27 the Korean War ends.	President Eisenhower presents his Domino Theory. The Senate censures Senator McCarthy for his abusive attacks. In *Brown v. Board of Education of Topeka, Kansas,* the United States Supreme Court rules against segregation by race in public schools.
The first "Walk, Don't Walk" signs are installed in Times Square, New York. The first 3-D movies are shown in theaters. *American Bandstand* debuts on local television in Philadelphia. It features music and dancing for teens. The Holiday Inn hotel chain is founded. The first issue of *Mad Magazine* goes on sale.	Kellogg's introduces Sugar Smacks cereal. Sara Lee Kitchens markets frozen cakes and pies. C. A. Swanson and Sons introduce the frozen TV dinner. Chevrolet introduces the Corvette, a two seat sports car.	Elvis Presley makes his first record. The Academy Awards are televised for the first time. Putt-Putt miniature golf courses are invented by Don Clayton. Twenty-six American publishers agree to regulate the contents of comic books.
Buckminster Fuller's geodesic dome is displayed. On November 1 the United States explodes the first hydrogen bomb in the South Pacific.	Jackie Cochran is the first woman to break the sound barrier. Dr. Jonas Salk develops a polio vaccine. Crik and Watson discover DNA. The aerosol valve is invented. The Nike Ajax is America's first surface-to-air missile. "Atomic Annie," a nuclear heavy artillery shell, is tested by the Army.	The polio vaccine is given to school children for the first time. The Navy launches the *Nautilus,* its first nuclear-powered submarine. The first transistor radio is marketed. Bell laboratories announces the photovoltaic cell which converts sunlight to electricity.

Time Line (cont.)

1955	1956	1957
Rosa Parks refuses to give up her seat on a bus; the Montgomery bus boycott follows.	Dwight D. Eisenhower is reelected.	President Eisenhower sends Army troops to Little Rock, Arkansas, to enforce integration of Central High School.
Martin Luther King, Jr., organizes demonstrations to demand civil rights for blacks.	The United States Supreme Court rules segregation in public schools is unconstitutional.	The Vietnam war begins.
The AFL and CIO merge.	The Federal Highway Act provides money to build an interstate highway system.	The Civil Rights Act of 1957 is passed in spite of Strom Thurmond's 24-hour fillibuster against it.
There are 16 women serving in the United States House of Representatives and one woman senator. A woman is also a non-voting observer from Hawaii.	Soviet tanks crush an uprising in Hungary.	
	In a dispute over the Suez Canal, Israeli-Anglo-French forces invade Egypt's Gaza Strip.	
Ray Kroc opens his first franchised McDonald's restaurant in Des Plaines, Illinois.	American actress Grace Kelly marries Prince Rainier III of Monaco.	Edsels are marketed by Ford.
"Rock Around the Clock" is the first rock and roll song to hit the charts.	The Platters become the first black singing group to have a song in the Top Ten.	Dr. Seuss' first book, *The Cat in the Hat*, is published.
Walt Disney presents the *Mickey Mouse Club*, a children's television program.	The first American edition of the *Guiness Book of World Records* is published.	Jim Henson's Muppets make their first national appearance on Steve Allen's *Tonight Show*.
On July 17 Disneyland opens in Anaheim, California.	Folk singer Pete Seeger is cited for contempt by the House Unamerican Affairs Committee.	Jack Kerouac publishes *On the Road*.
Marian Anderson becomes the first African American to sing a leading role with the Metropolitan Opera in New York.	Japanese pick-up trucks are imported to America for the first time.	
	Martin Luther King, Jr.'s, home is bombed.	
Multiple track recording is introduced, leading to commercial stereophonic records and equipment.	Dr. Albert Sabin announces the development of an oral polio vaccine.	Russia launches *Sputnik I* and *II*. Laika becomes the first animal in space in *Sputnik II*.
	Procter and Gamble introduces Crest, the first fluoride toothpaste.	Hoover markets the first spin dryer for clothes.
	Heezen and Ewing discover the Mid-Oceanic Ridge, a formation of mountains and rifts that circles the Earth under the oceans.	The first Intercontinental Ballistic Missile(ICBM) is developed.
	Bell Labs introduces a transistorized computer, "The Leprechaun."	
	FORTRAN, a computer-software language, is introduced.	

Time Line *(cont.)*

	Politics and Economics	Social and Cultural	Science and Technology
1959	On January 3 Alaska becomes the 49th state. On August 21 Hawaii becomes the 50th state. Soviet Premier Khrushchev rejects President Eisenhower's proposal to end tests of nuclear weapons.	Barbie dolls are introduced by Mattel, Inc., on March 1. The latest fad among collegians is stuffing as many people as possible into a phone booth. The Guggenheim Museum, designed by architect Frank Lloyd Wright, opens in New York.	The Mercury Project is created to launch Americans into space. Xerox introduces the first commercial copier. The St. Lawrence Seaway, which connects the St. Lawrence River to the Great Lakes, opens. Sony produces the first black and white transistorized television.
1958	The National Defense Education Act provides funding for more science education in schools. NASA is formed. Robert H. W. Welch founds the John Birch Society, an ultraconservative anticommunist group.	Fifteen-year-old chess player Bobby Fischer earns the title of International Grand Master in chess. Hula-Hoops make their debut. Jet service to Europe begins. Alvin Ailey is the first African American to head a dance company. Pizza Hut opens its first restaurant in Kansas City, Missouri. Elvis Presley is inducted into the Army.	The first United States artificial satellite orbits the Earth. *Explorer I* is launched by the United States. The *Nautilus* submarine goes under the North Pole ice cap. *Explorer IV* verifies the existence of a radiation belt surrounding the planet. The belt is named the Van Allen Radiation Belt.

Using the Time Line

Use pages five to eight to create a visual display for your classroom. Follow the steps outlined below to assemble the time line as a bulletin board display and then choose from the suggested uses those that best suit your classroom needs.

Bulletin Board Assembly

Copy pages five to eight. Enlarge and/or color them, if desired. Tape the pages together to form a continuous time line and attach it to a prepared bulletin board background or a classroom wall. (To make a reusable bulletin board, glue each page of the time line to oaktag. After the glue has dried, laminate them. Write on the laminated pages with dry-erase markers.)

	1950	1951	1952	1953	1954	1955	1956	1957	1958	1959	
Politics and Economics	The Korean war begins when North Korea crosses the 38th parallel into South Korea on June 25. Senator Joseph McCarthy begins his hunt for communists.	The Rosenbergs are executed for spying against the United States. General MacArthur is relieved of his post by President Truman. The 22nd Amendment is passed; it limits the president to two terms. Congress passes the Mutual Security Act, authorizing almost $8 million in foreign aid.	Dwight D. Eisenhower is elected to the presidency; Richard Nixon is his vice-president. Puerto Rico becomes the first United States commonwealth.	Eisenhower is inaugurated as the 34th president; Richard Nixon is his vice-president. Earl Warren becomes Chief Justice of the Supreme Court. On July 27 the Korean War ends.	President Eisenhower presents his Domino Theory. The Senate censures Senator McCarthy for his abusive attacks. In Brown v. Board of Education of Topeka, Kansas, the United States Supreme Court rules against segregation by race in public schools.	Rosa Parks refuses to give up her seat on a bus; the Montgomery bus boycott follows. Martin Luther King, Jr., organizes demonstrations to demand civil rights for blacks. The AFL and CIO merge. There are 16 women serving in the United States House of Representatives and one woman senator. A woman is also a non-voting observer from Hawaii.	The United States Supreme Court rules segregation in public schools is unconstitutional. The Federal Highway Act provides money to build an interstate highway system. Soviet tanks crush an uprising in Hungary. In a dispute over the Suez Canal, Israeli-Anglo-French forces invade Egypt's Gaza Strip.	President Eisenhower sends Army troops to Little Rock, Arkansas, to enforce integration of Central High School. The Vietnam war begins.	The National Defense Education Act provides funding for more science education in schools. NASA is formed. Robert H. W. Welch founds the John Birch Society, an ultraconservative anticommunist group.	On January 3 Alaska becomes the 49th state. On August 21 Hawaii becomes the 50th state. Soviet Premier Khrushchev rejects President Eisenhower's proposal to end tests of nuclear weapons. The Civil Rights Act of 1959 is passed in spite of Strom Thurmond's 24-hour filibuster against it.	**Politics and Economics**
Social and Cultural	The Peanuts comic strip is first published. Smokey the Bear becomes the symbol of forest fire safety. The Adventures of Superman starring George Reeves debuts on television. Betty Crocker's Picture Cookbook is published. The Henry J., a compact car, is introduced by Henry J. Kaiser. Minute Rice is introduced in supermarkets. The Nobel Peace Prize is awarded to United States diplomat Ralph J. Bunche, an African American. CBS television airs Colorcast, a commercial color transmission that stars Ed Sullivan and Arthur Godfrey.	Levittown, the first planned suburb, opens in New York. On October 5 I Love Lucy premieres on television.	The first "Walk, Don't Walk" signs are installed in Times Square, New York. Velcro, a new material, is shown in theaters. American Bandstand debuts on local television in Philadelphia. It features music and dancing for teens. The Holiday Inn hotel chain is founded. The first issue of Mad Comics goes on sale.	Kellogg's introduces Sugar Smacks cereal. Aunt Lee Kitchens markets frozen cakes and pies. C. A. Swanson and Sons introduce the frozen TV dinner. Chevrolet introduces the Corvette, a two-seat sports car.	Elvis Presley makes his first record. The Academy Awards are televised for the first time. Putt-Putt miniature golf courses are invented by Don Clayton. Twenty-six American publishers agree to regulate the contents of comic books.	Ray Kroc opens his first franchised McDonald's restaurant in Des Plaines, Illinois. "Rock Around the Clock" is the first rock and roll song to hit the charts. Walt Disney presents the Mickey Mouse Club, a children's television program.	American actress Grace Kelly marries Prince Rainier III of Monaco. The Platters become the first black singing group to have a song in the Top Ten. The first American edition of the Guinness Book of World Records is published. Folk singer Pete Seeger is cited for contempt by the House Unamerican Affairs Committee. Japanese pick-up trucks are imported to America for the first time. Martin Luther King, Jr.'s, home is bombed.	Fifteen-year-old chess player Bobby Fischer earns the title of International Grand Master in chess. Hula-Hoops make their debut. Jim Henson's Muppets make their first national appearance on Steve Allen's Tonight Show. Jack Kerouac publishes On the Road.	Darlie dolls are introduced by Mattel, Inc., on March 1. His sister sat among colleagues is scuttling as many people as possible into a phone booth. The Guggenheim Museum, designed by architect Frank Lloyd Wright, opens in New York.	**Social and Cultural**
Science and Technology	The first kidney transplant operation is performed.	The United States explodes an atomic bomb underground for the first time at Frenchmen Flats, Nevada. UNIVAC I is the first electronic digital computer to be sold commercially. Electricity is first generated from atomic energy.	Buckminster Fuller's geodesic dome is displayed. On November 1 the United States explodes the first hydrogen bomb, in the South Pacific.	Dr. Jonas Salk develops a vaccine to guard against polio. Crick and Watson discover DNA. The aerosol valve is invented. The Nike missile is America's first surface-to-air missile. "Atomic Annie," a nuclear heavy artillery shell, is tested by the Army.	The polio vaccine is given to school children for the first time. The Navy launches the Nautilus, its first atomic-powered submarine. The first transistor radio is marketed. Soil laboratories announces the photovoltaic cell which converts sunlight to electricity.	Multiple track recording is introduced, leading to commercial stereophonic records and equipment.	Procter and Gamble introduces Crest, the first fluoride toothpaste. Heezen and Ewing discover the Mid-Oceanic Ridge, a formation of mountains and rifts that circles the Earth under the oceans. Bell Labs introduces a transistorized computer, "The Leprechaun." FORTRAN, a computer-software language, is introduced.	Russia launches Sputnik I. The first intercontinental ballistic missile (ICBM) is developed.	The first United States artificial satellite orbits the Earth. Explorer I is launched by the United States. The Nautilus submarine goes under the North Pole ice cap. Explorer IV verifies the existence of a radiation belt surrounding the planet. The belt is named the Van Allen Radiation Belt.	The Mercury Project is created to launch Americans into space. Xerox introduces the first commercial copier. The St. Lawrence Seaway, which connects the St. Lawrence River to the Great Lakes, opens. Sony produces the first black and white transistorized television.	**Science and Technology**

Suggested Uses

1. Use the time line to assess students' initial knowledge of the era. Construct a web to find out what they know about the Korean War or the Montgomery bus boycott, for example. Find out what they would like to know. Plan your lessons accordingly.

2. Assign each group of students a specific year. As they research that year, let them add pictures, names, and events to the appropriate area of the time line.

3. Assign the students to find out what events were happening around the world during the 1950s. Tell them to add that information to the bottom of the time line.

4. After adding new names, places, and events to the time line, use the information gathered as a study guide for assessment. Base your quizzes and exams on those people, places, and events which you have studied.

5. After the time line has been on display for a few days, begin to quiz students about the people, places, and events named on the time line. Call on one student at a time to stand so that he or she is facing away from the actual time line. Ask a question based on the information. *Variation:* Let the students compose the questions.

6. Use the time line as a springboard for class discussions, for example: Why is the Korean War called the "forgotten war"? What events led up to the Korean War? What was the impact of television on family life? What toys invented during the fifties are still popular today? What inventions of the fifties are now obsolete?

7. Divide the students into three groups and assign each group a different area: politics/economics, social/cultural, and science/technology. Have each group brainstorm important related people, places, and events that occurred during the fifties, and then create a group mural depicting these important happenings. Get permission to decorate a hallway wall or tape several sheets of butcher paper together to make a giant canvas.

8. Assign groups of students to make specialized time lines, for example, a time line of inventions, a time line of events in the civil rights movement, or a time line of the Korean War events.

Fifties Overview

- After World War II Korea was divided in two along the 38th parallel. The country was supposed to be reunited after free elections, but the communists, who controlled the North, would not allow the elections to take place. On June 25, 1950, Kim Il Sung directed his North Korean forces to cross into South Korea. President Truman, who was determined to keep communism from expanding into other regions, had the United States lead the United Nations-directed response. Fighting was not easy in Korea, and over 33,000 American lives were lost before the war ended in 1953.

- Elsewhere, the Cold War continued, with the United States pledging support to its former Allies. The Soviet Union entered alliances with China and Eastern European countries.

- The nuclear arms race, which began in late 1949 when the Soviets successfully tested an atomic bomb, also continued. The U.S. exploded the first hydrogen bomb, 500 times more powerful than the previous atomic bombs, in 1952. In less than a year the Soviets tested a similar weapon. The threat of these technologies added to the Cold War tension between the U.S. and the Soviets. In America, public and private bomb shelters were built.

- Concerned by the spread of communism in Europe and Asia, some feared it would take over the world and worried about communist subversion in the United States. Senator Joseph McCarthy led the "Red Scare," accusing hundreds of innocent people and ruining their lives. Finally he was condemned by his fellow senators, and he quickly lost favor.

- The Supreme Court ruled in 1954 against segregation by race in public schools. In 1955 Rosa Parks's refusal to give up her seat on the bus for a white person sparked the Montgomery bus boycott. The boycott ended a year later with the Supreme Court decision that segregation on buses was unconstitutional. In 1957 in Little Rock, Arkansas, National Guard troops attempted to block the admission of nine black students to a previously all-white school, Central High School. The Guard was removed by an order from the Supreme Court, and 1,000 Army paratroopers escorted the students to their high school. The fight for civil rights continued throughout this and the next decades.

- In 1957 the Russians launched the first artificial satellite, *Sputnik I*. American scientists scrambled to compete in the space race.

- Teen idols like James Dean and Marlon Brando were featured in films. Bill Haley's "Rock Around the Clock" heralded a new era in popular music—rock and roll. Buddy Holly, Little Richard, and Jerry Lee Lewis were popular with teens, but Elvis Presley soon eclipsed all of them.

- Television came into more and more homes during the fifties, changing the traditional lifestyle and family structure. People ate TV dinners while perched around the television. New programs depicted ideal family images. Real events could be seen almost as soon as they happened.

- Women were encouraged to stay at home and to take care of their families. Many lived in the suburbs in tracts of similar houses.

For Discussion

1. What effect did the space race have on education in U.S. public schools?

2. What were Elvis Presley's contributions to American music?

3. How did television impact the American family?

Introducing the Fifties

On this page you will find some interesting ways to introduce the fifties to the students. Keep in mind that these are suggestions only and it is not necessary to use all of them. Your project selections should be based on student needs, interests, and objectives.

1. **Display** Create a special display table with any or all of the following products: Crest fluoride toothpaste, White-Out, a Frisbee, 3-D glasses, WD-40, a Barbie doll, Jif peanut butter, *Mad Magazine*, and a TV dinner (box only). Place a tent sign reading "Guess when each item on this table was invented" on the table, and provide a box for student responses. After a few days check the answers with the whole group.

2. **Contests** Hula-Hoops and Frisbee-throwing were both big crazes during the fifties. Conduct a contest to see who can spin the most Hula-Hoops at once, or have a Frisbee throwing festival to see which pair can toss and catch the Frisbee the farthest.

3. **TV Reviews** Show a video of a typical 1950s family drama or sit-com, like *Leave It to Beaver*, *Father Knows Best*, etc., to the class. Discuss how each family member is portrayed. Ask students if this family is realistic to them. Have them compare the TV family to their own family.

4. *Peanuts* The *Peanuts* comic strip debuted in 1950. Make copies of several different *Peanuts* cartoons; cover up the dialogue before copying. Distribute the copies to student pairs and instruct them to write new dialogue for each comic strip.

5. **Fast Food** Ray Kroc, a restaurant equipment salesman, received an order for eight shake mixers from Mac and Dick McDonald for their San Bernadino, California, restaurant. Amazed by the quantity (one machine could make five shakes at a time), Kroc visited the brothers. Impressed by the efficiency, popularity, and profitability of the operation, he purchased a franchise and started his own McDonald's Restaurant in Chicago in 1955. Kroc followed the principles of the brothers, using their assembly-line process of food production. When Kroc bought out the McDonald brothers in 1961, he owned 100 restaurants. The rest is history. Since then numerous others have sought to imitate their methods. With the class, brainstorm some other famous fast food restaurants. Let the students vote for their favorite fast food restaurant and use the data gathered to make pie graphs or picture graphs. Complete the McDonald's math activity on page 13.

6. **Fifties Art** Famous artists of the fifties included Jasper Johns and Frank Lloyd Wright. Have the students create some fifties art with the projects on pages 56 and 57.

7. **Rock and Roll** Read the information on pages 58 and 59. Ask the students which rock and roll music artists are familiar to them. Play some fifties rock and roll music and let students rate each song on the rating form on page 59.

8. **A Fifties Day** Direct the students to research what clothing was popular with teens during the 1950s and then specify a day on which they come to school in fifties garb. Eat TV dinners for lunch. Play with Frisbees and Hula-Hoops. Dance to fifties music. Supply each pair or small group with a paint-by-number kit to complete.

Discussing the Fifties

Create student interest with a lively discussion. Suggested topics and some methods for implementing them follow.

A Woman's Place During the fifties, the prevailing philosophy was that a woman's place was in the home caring for her husband and children. Ask students to brainstorm some pros and cons of this position; have them defend their answers.

Forgotten War The Korean War has often been referred to as the "forgotten war". Discuss with students how this title originated and why the Korean War remains in the background of United States history.

DNA One of the most important scientific breakthroughs of the decade occurred when Crick and Watson developed a model for DNA. Discuss with the class why DNA is important. Have them look for current newspaper and magazine articles to see how it is being used in crime detection and genetics.

Civil Rights During the fifties the civil rights movement was just beginning. Rosa Parks's refusal to give up her bus seat for a white man sparked a whole new battle for equality. Tell students that they are Parks's attorney and have them explain to the judge why Parks should be cleared of all charges.

Space Race When Russia launched *Sputnik I*, Americans were caught off guard. The event showed how seriously America lagged in space technology. Not wanting to be outdone, agencies were created to work on future United States spacecraft. The government also allocated millions of dollars to be spent on scientific education in schools at all levels. Discuss how more science instruction would help the future space program.

McCarthyism Senator Joseph McCarthy started a one-man war on communism. He wrongfully accused innocent people and caused thousands to lose their jobs. Pair the students for some role-playing. One partner is McCarthy, while the other is the accused communist. First McCarthy explains the charges, and then the other partner defends himself or herself.

Fifty States Both Alaska and Hawaii became states in 1959. As a class discuss the natural resources of each state. Group the students and assign each group either Alaska or Hawaii. Direct them to write a 1950s TV ad whose message tells why the state should be admitted to the union.

Campaign '52 Dwight David Eisenhower was a former career military man with no political party while Stevenson was a governor, a Democrat, and well-spoken. Ask the students to explain who they think was the better choice for president. Tell them to defend their views.

Spying In 1951 the Rosenbergs were executed for spying against the United States. Historians still argue over their guilt or innocence. After students research the story of the Rosenbergs, conduct a class debate in which they discuss evidence to support guilt or innocence.

McDonald's Math

The data in the box below is taken from dietary sheets provided by McDonald's restaurants. Read through the data box and use the information provided to figure out which side of each inequality has the greater number of calories. Place a < or > sign on the line to complete each inequality.

Data

These figures reflect the number of calories in each item.

 hamburger—270

 cheeseburger—320

 fish sandwich—360

 small french fries—210

garden salad—80

 hot fudge sundae—290

 apple pie—260

 1% milk—100

 small cola—150

 chocolate shake—340

1. 2 hamburgers _____ 2 hot fudge sundaes

2. 1 fish sandwich _____ 4 garden salads

3. 5 small colas _____ 3 fish sandwiches

4. 3 chocolate shakes _____ 12 1% milks

5. 2 apple pies _____ 7 garden salads

6. 3 cheeseburgers _____ 5 small french fries

7. 2 garden salads + 3 cheeseburgers _____ 4 hamburgers

8. 4 fish sandwiches _____ 6 small french fries + 1 garden salad

9. 3 small colas + 1 chocolate shake _____ 2 apple pies + 3 1% milks

10. 2 hot fudge sundaes _____ 2 small french fries + 3 garden salads

11. 6 1% milks + 2 cheeseburgers _____ 4 small french fries + 1 shake

12. 3 apple pies + 2 fish sandwiches _____ 3 cheeseburgers + 3 small french fries

In the space below write two more inequalities using the data from the box above.

1. _____

2. _____

1950s Legislation

Some important Supreme Court decisions and a number of important pieces of legislation were ratified in the fifties. An outline of some of these measures is provided below.

McCarran Act On September 9, 1950, Congress passed the Internal Security Act sponsored by Senator Patrick McCarran of Nevada. It allowed the government to maintain close control over all communists and their activities in this country. The bill supported Senator Joseph McCarthy's anticommunist campaign.

22nd Amendment This Constitutional Amendment was ratified in 1951 and prohibited the president from serving more than two terms.

Brown v. Board of Education On May 17, 1954, the Supreme Court handed down its decision in Brown v. the Board of Education of Topeka. The law on which the South had maintained its segregated school system was struck down. The court determined that the doctrine of separate but equal was unconstitutional. States were ordered to integrate their schools, but many tried every way they could to block the ruling. In 1957 President Eisenhower ordered a U.S. Army unit to Little Rock to escort black students to Central High School.

Federal Highway Act This 1956 legislation provided billions of dollars to construct a modern interstate highway system. As more and more people began driving to work and the production of cars increased, it was necessary to build an up-to-date network of roads.

Segregation on Buses In December of 1956, the Supreme Court handed down their ruling about segregation on buses. Following Rosa Parks's 1955 arrest, Martin Luther King, Jr., led a boycott of Montgomery buses. For thirteen months they continued the boycott until the Supreme Court ruled that segregation on Alabama buses was unconstitutional.

Civil Rights Act of 1957 The 1957 civil rights bill was passed on August 30 of that year. Although it provided for equal rights for African Americans, it was a weak measure. Senator Strom Thurmond filibustered for 24 hours to hold up its passage. He predicted that the South would strongly resist its provisions.

National Defense Education Act The Russian-launched *Sputnik I* on October 4, 1957, caused some panic in the U.S. Worried that American scientists were falling dangerously behind the Soviet Union in missile technology, Congress funded $887 million dollars to improve science education in both high schools and colleges. This bill was passed on August 23, 1958.

Suggested Activities

Numbered Highways Investigate how U.S. highways are numbered. Each group of students can use a road atlas of the U.S. See if you can determine any strategy to the numbering of highways. For a more complete explanation of the system, see *The Handy Science Answer Book* published by Visible Ink Press, 1994.

Impact Discuss the impact on society today of the above-named legislative acts and Supreme Court decisions.

Land of the Midnight Sun

In 1867 William Seward purchased Alaska for the United States, but the territory did not become a state until January 3, 1959. On the map below you will find more facts about the 49th state. Notice that some important information is missing. Research the names of the places and label the map at the corresponding numbers.

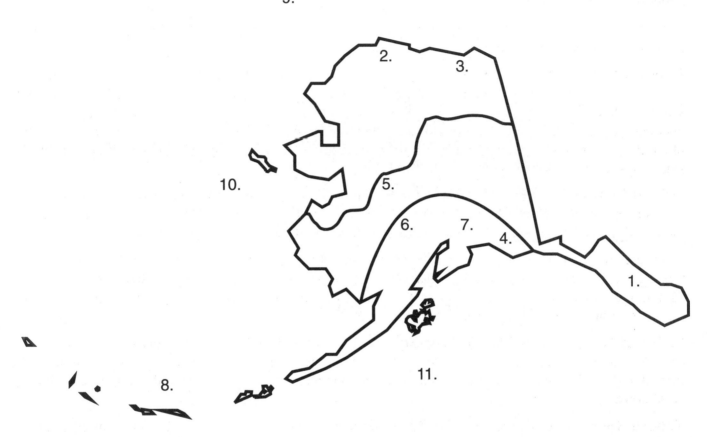

Alaska is the largest of the 50 states. Two important cities are (1)_____, its capital, and (2)_____, the northernmost point in the United States. From (3)_____ to (4)_____ the Alaska pipeline extends 800 miles north to south. The (5)_____ River runs from east to west, almost through the center of the state's vast expanse. The (6)_____ mountains are home to (7)_____, the tallest peak in all of North America. A chain of islands, the (8)_____ Islands, extends west from Alaska toward Russia. In all, Alaska's coastline exceeds that of all the other states combined with the (9)_____ Ocean to the north, (10)_____ Sea to the west, and the (11)_____ Ocean to the south.

Challenge: Write a report about the great state of Alaska. Include these topics: its capital, area, and population; state motto, bird, flower, tree, and song; important physical features; industry and economy; culture; geography of the state; history of the area.

Aloha!

Like Alaska, Hawaii is not connected to the rest of the United States. Instead, it is a group of islands located in the Pacific Ocean southwest of the U.S. mainland. Once an independent kingdom, on August 21, 1959, Hawaii became the 50th state. To learn more about the islands that compose Hawaii, label the eight islands pictured below. Then research and write the correct islands for the following clues.

1. _____ Honolulu, the capital city of Hawaii, is located here. It is also home to the Pearl Harbor Memorial. Eighty percent of all Hawaiians live on this island.

2. _____ Years ago Father Damien established a leper colony here. It is called the Friendly Island and contains a dry plateau, as well as rugged mountains and dry canyons.

3. _____ The largest island, it is home to the Kilauea volcano.

4. _____ Of the eight main Hawaiian islands, it was formed first. Mount Waialeale on this island is the rainiest spot in the world. It is called the Garden Island and is almost circular in shape.

5. _____ Often called the Valley Island, many canyons cut through its two volcanic mountains. Haleakala, a massive dormant volcano, can be found here.

6. _____ The smallest of the eight main islands, it has no permanent inhabitants. Until 1993, it was used by the Navy as a bombing range.

7. _____ Known as the Pineapple Island, it is owned by the Dole Company.

8. _____ This island, known as the Forbidden Island, is privately owned and is home to a huge cattle ranch.

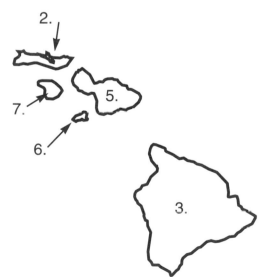

Answers (Fold under before copying)

1. Oahu 2. Molokai 3. Hawaii 4. Kauai 5. Maui 6. Kahoolawe 7. Lanai 8. Niihau

The Rosenbergs and McCarthy

When Americans learned that the Russians had exploded an atomic bomb in September of 1949, the news sent shock waves throughout the nation. Now that another country had the A-bomb, American security was gravely threatened. Millions of Americans worried about protecting themselves and installed bomb shelters in their backyards. Students in school were regularly drilled on what to do in case of a nuclear attack.

Ethel and Julius Rosenberg

The question next turned to how the Russians had obtained the information to build an atomic bomb. Many Americans believed that Russia did not have the capability of producing such a weapon themselves and assumed that Russia somehow must have learned U.S. secrets. A wave of hysteria was touched off when Dr. Klaus Fuchs, a British physicist, confessed to giving atomic bomb secrets to the Soviet Union. Alger Hiss, a high-ranking official in the State Department, was accused of passing important secrets to communist spies. These cases set the stage for the most sensational spy case of the century. In 1951 Julius and Ethel Rosenberg were charged with treason for plotting to arrange for the transfer of atomic secrets to the Soviet Union during World War II. Ethel's brother, David Greenglass, had been spying for the Soviets, and he named the couple as leaders of his spy ring. Even though the charges were never proven, the Rosenbergs were prosecuted and sentenced to death.

Joseph McCarthy

After the trial the Justice Department began taking drastic measures to protect the U.S. against communist subversion. Loyalty oaths were required for jobs that had nothing to do with national security, and President Truman authorized investigations into the backgrounds of all federal employees. Senator Joseph McCarthy of Wisconsin, a little-known Republican senator, led the Red Scare that was to sweep the country by announcing that he had a list of people working for the State Department who were members of the Communist party. Although he never produced this list of Communists, he continued to make even more irresponsible accusations. In the process he destroyed the reputations of many innocent persons, including hundreds of film directors and actors who were blacklisted because of these accusations. Even members of his own staff came under attack. McCarthy met his match, however, when he tackled the U.S. Army. As a result of those hearings, the Senate voted to condemn Senator McCarthy for his abusive actions. His influence quickly declined, but the term "McCarthyism" came to be synonymous with the character assassination that he carried out.

Suggested Activities

Research Research the facts of the Rosenberg trial and find out the evidence against them. Was it enough to convict them, and did the punishment fit the supposed crime?

Witch Hunts Discuss some other witch hunts that have been carried out in American history (Salem witch hunts, Red Scare of the 1920s).

Literature Arthur Miller wrote his classic play *The Crucible* in the shadow of McCarthyism. Read the play and discuss its historic, as well as its modern, significance.

Harry S. Truman

33rd President, 1945–1953

Harry S. Truman

Vice President: Alben W. Barkley

Born: May 8, 1884, in Lamar, Missouri

Died: December 26, 1972

Party: Democrat

Parents: John Anderson Truman and Martha Ellen Young

First Lady: Elizabeth (Bess) Virginia Wallace

Child: Margaret

Nickname: Man from Independence

Famous Firsts:

- He was the first president to take office during wartime.
- He was the first president to travel underwater in a modern submarine and was the first and only president to use the atomic bomb on another country.

Achievements:

- He was elected to the U.S. Senate in 1934 and reelected in 1940.
- Truman represented the U.S. at the signing of the United Nations' charter in June 1945.
- He signed the NATO treaty for mutual defense among 12 nations.
- On March 13, 1947, Truman issued his policy for "containment" of Communism, later called the Truman Doctrine.
- When the Soviets blockaded West Berlin in 1948, Truman ordered an airlift to the city. Constant shuttles kept the West Berliners supplied with food, coal, and necessities.
- His Fair Deal increased Social Security benefits, raised the minimum wage from 40 cents to 75 cents per hour, and appropriated money for constructing low-income housing.
- He fired General MacArthur after MacArthur publicly voiced his unhappiness with Truman's refusal to allow a war with China.
- Truman began the fight to integrate schools.
- He appointed the first African American federal judge.
- He ended segregation in the army, navy, and marines.

Interesting Facts:

- Truman served as an artillery officer in World War I.
- He kept a sign on his desk that read, "The buck stops here." Truman was known for his feisty character and occasional use of foul language.
- As a child he had to wear thick glasses. Because the glasses were expensive, he was not allowed to play contact sports and took piano lessons instead.
- After serving in World War I, he opened a men's clothing store in Kansas City.
- In the 1948 election, the *Chicago Tribune* ran a headline, "Dewey Defeats Truman." However, Truman won the election.
- He did not have a middle name. The S was only an initial.

Dwight D. Eisenhower

34th President, 1953–1961

Vice President: Richard M. Nixon
Born: October 14, 1890, in Denison, Texas
Died: March 28, 1969
Party: Republican
Parents: David Jacob Eisenhower, Ida Elizabeth Stover
First Lady: Mamie Geneva Doud
Children: Dwight, John
Nickname: Ike
Education: Graduate of West Point Academy
Famous Firsts:

Dwight D. Eisenhower

- Eisenhower was the first president to have a putting green installed on the White House lawn.
- His 1956 election marked the first time since 1848 that a president had failed to carry at least one house of Congress for his party.
- He was the first president of all fifty states.
- Eisenhower was the first licensed pilot and the first five-star general elected to the office of president.

Achievements:

- Eisenhower made good on a campaign promise and ended the Korean War.
- In 1953 he appointed Earl Warren, considered to be a moderate, as the new chief justice. Warren led a revolution on the Court when he reversed an 1896 separate-but-equal doctrine.
- He went to Korea to revive the stalled peace talks.

Interesting Facts:

- When he was born, Eisenhower's given name was David Dwight. Later, he switched his first and middle names.
- His mother was a pacifist and cried when he decided to attend West Point.
- Eisenhower ranked 65th in his class of 165 at West Point.
- A professional soldier, he helped General MacArthur break up the Bonus March during the thirties.
- He was the only president to have served in both world wars.
- During World War II, Eisenhower served as the supreme Allied commander.
- When Eisenhower was first approached to run for president, he did not have a political party. The Democrats courted him in 1948, but his views were closer to Republican ideas.
- President Eisenhower's favorite sport was golf, and he could often be found on the White House lawn practicing chip shots.
- Eisenhower also enjoyed painting.
- An accomplished cook, vegetable soup and cornmeal pancakes were two of Eisenhower's best dishes.
- Eisenhower was the last president born in the nineteenth century.
- At the time, Eisenhower was the oldest man ever elected as president.

Bess and Mamie

Bess Truman was more than happy to give up her role as first lady in 1953 and to turn the position over to Mamie Eisenhower. Both were gracious hostesses, and both relished their privacy. Yet the two were very different in other respects. Find out more about these first ladies. Read each description below and then circle the correct first lady at the beginning of each phrase. Use history books, biographies, encyclopedias, and other reference materials to help you find the correct answers.

Bess Truman

Mamie Eisenhower

1. **Bess   Mamie** moved 28 times as husband changed assignments

2. **Bess   Mamie** husband was a career military man

3. **Bess   Mamie** the longest-lived first lady in American history

4. **Bess   Mamie** made few public appearances

5. **Bess   Mamie** had one daughter, Margaret

6. **Bess   Mamie** born in Boone, Iowa

7. **Bess   Mamie** trademark color was pink

8. **Bess   Mamie** was 60 years old when she became first lady

9. **Bess   Mamie** liked to watch "As the World Turns" on TV

10. **Bess   Mamie** husband referred to her as "the Boss" in public

11. **Bess   Mamie** born in Independence, Missouri

12. **Bess   Mamic** first met future husband in Sunday School

13. **Bess   Mamie** loved to entertain and was a popular hostess

14. **Bess   Mamie** born in November of 1896

15. **Bess   Mamie** was frugal and practical like her husband

16. **Bess   Mamie** met her future husband in San Antonio

17. **Bess   Mamie** adopted no causes as first lady

18. **Bess   Mamie** died in 1979

19. **Bess   Mamie** moved to Blair House during White House renovation

20. **Bess   Mamie** born in 1885

21. **Bess   Mamie** had a son who died in infancy

22. **Bess   Mamie** had a daughter who tried to launch a singing career

23. **Bess   Mamie** distributed buttons as White House souvenirs

24. **Bess   Mamie** was a late riser; she conducted business from her bed

25. **Bess   Mamie** had a grandson who married a future president's daughter

Challenge: On the back of this paper, construct a Venn diagram to show the likenesses and differences between these two first ladies. Add two more facts to each category.

Election Facts and Figures

	Election of 1952	Election of 1956
Democrats	Adlai Stevenson, governor of Illinois and grandson of President Grover Cleveland's vice-president, was drafted by his party and agreed to run. Senator John Sparkman of Alabama, a liberal on most issues except civil rights, was chosen as the vice-presidential candidate.	Once again, Adlai Stevenson decided to run despite his failed bid four years earlier. This time, Senator Estes Kefauver from Tennessee became his running mate. Kefauver was known for his fight against government corruption.
Republicans	General Dwight D. Eisenhower, a popular U.S. figure, was the Republican candidate. Although Eisenhower had been approached by both political parties, he chose to run as a Republican. Anticommunist crusader Richard M. Nixon of California was his running mate.	The Eisenhower-Nixon ticket was left intact.
Slogans	The Republicans printed "I Like Ike" on buttons, nail files, makeup cases, stockings, and other women's items which were distributed throughout the campaign.	
Issues	A strong national defense was at the core of the Republican platform. They felt that Eisenhower symbolized the strength of the military and criticized the Democratic policy of appeasement of communism. In their platform the Democrats called for more civil rights for blacks.	Eisenhower's health worried both Republicans and Democrats. He had suffered a moderate heart attack in 1955 and had intestinal surgery in 1956. However, the Democrats chose not to raise the health issues for fear of offending voters.
Winner	Eisenhower won the election with 33,936,234 popular votes. He earned 442 electoral votes to Stevenson's 89.	Eisenhower-Nixon won with almost 2 million more popular votes than they had received in the previous election. Once again, the House of Representatives and the Senate remained Democratic. This marked the first time since Zachary Taylor's election in 1848 that a president had been unable to carry at least one house of Congress for his party.

An Election Challenge

Fill in the missing 1952 and 1956 election figures by working the problems in each sentence below. Write the answers in the correct section of the chart. Then use the information in the completed chart to figure out answers to the questions on page 23.

Year	Candidate	Popular Vote	Electoral Vote
1952	Dwight D. Eisenhower		
	Adlai Stevenson		
1956	Dwight D. Eisenhower		
	Adlai Stevenson		

1. In 1952 Eisenhower had (83,185,702 - 49,249,468)_____popular votes.

2. Stevenson earned (32,485 ÷ 365)_____electoral votes in 1952.

3. Eisenhower had (25,636 ÷ 58)_____electoral votes in 1952.

4. In 1952 Stevenson had (31,086,057 - 3,771,065)_____popular votes.

5. In 1956 Stevenson received (6,263,754 + 19,758,998)_____popular votes.

6. The number of electoral votes Eisenhower received in 1956 was (39,302 ÷ 86)_____

7. In 1956 Eisenhower received (16,746,857 + 18,843,615)_____popular votes.

8. Stevenson received (31,317 ÷ 429)_____electoral votes in 1956.

Challenge: Altogether there are _____ popular votes in the 1952 election and _____ popular votes in the 1956 election.

An Election Challenge *(cont.)*

Use the election facts and figures below and on the previous page (page 22) to help you complete the activities below.

Math Problems

1. In the 1952 election Eisenhower had 442 electoral votes and Stevenson had 89. What percentage of the electoral votes did each candidate have?

2. In the 1956 election Eisenhower received 1,654,238 more popular votes than in the 1952 elections. How many total popular votes did he receive in 1956?

Mapping Exercise

During the 1952 election Eisenhower carried all the states except AR, LA, KY, GA, MS, AL, SC, NC, and WV. On the map below color all the states carried by the Republicans red. Color all the states carried by the Democrats blue.

For Discussion

1. During the 1956 election one issue was President Eisenhower's health, yet the Democrats chose not to use it against him for fear it would offend voters. Would an issue like that be withheld from voters today? How would you characterize campaigns in recent years?

2. Stevenson was well-known for his oratory skills. Eisenhower, however, avoided controversial issues and was not a good public speaker. Why, then, do you think that Eisenhower defeated Stevenson for the presidency?

Korean War Knowledge

Check students' knowledge of the Korean War with this pre-test. Copy the list of terms in the box below onto the chalkboard or overhead projector. Instruct the students to number a sheet of paper from one to twelve. Read one description at a time and allow students to choose an answer from the list. After all descriptions have been read, review the answers together.

Collect the papers and save them. Administer the test again after you have completed your Korean War studies. Compare the results of the pre- and post-tests to assess students' progress.

Note: Answers appear in parentheses after each statement for your easy reference.

Panmunjom	C-47	Operation Big Switch
Koje	Yalu River	38th Parallel
Pyongyang	Punchbowl	Operation Little Switch
Seoul	Inchon Landing	Kaesong

1. The site of very bloody fighting in 1951, it lies in a highly mountainous area north of the 38th parallel. *(Punchbowl)*

2. The first peace talks were conducted there. *(Kaesong)*

3. This was the name given to the exchange of prisoners of war in August 1953. *(Operation Big Switch)*

4. It is the capital city of North Korea. *(Pyongyang)*

5. This type of aircraft was used by UN forces to transport supplies and airlift wounded soldiers during the Korean War. *(C-47)*

6. The Chinese protected this border between Manchuria and North Korea from UN forces. *(Yalu River)*

7. Most of the peace talks which brought a final end to the Korean War were conducted here. *(Panmunjom)*

8. The UN forces landed behind the North Korean lines here on September 15, 1950. *(Inchon Landing)*

9. This code name was given to the exchange of sick and wounded prisoners of war in the spring of 1953. *(Operation Little Switch)*

10. Communist prisoners of war were kept by UN forces on this island off the coast of South Korea. *(Koje)*

11. At the end of World War II, the United States and the Soviet Union established this line to separate North Korea from South Korea. *(38th Parallel)*

12. The capital city of South Korea, it had been the capital of all of Korea before World War II. *(Seoul)*

A History of the Korean War

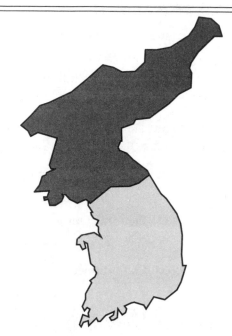

On this page you will find a brief overview of the Korean War. Expand your knowledge of the events preceding and following the war by exploring further any of the research topics at the bottom of the page.

Background Times were prosperous after World War II, yet there was a lingering hint of fear in the air. Many people believed the United States was filled with communists. Indeed, some communist spies were discovered here, the Rosenberg case being the most infamous example. (See page 17 for more about this couple.) There was also the question of the atomic bomb. The U.S. discovered it was no longer alone in this area when Russia tested an atomic bomb soon after the war. China was another threat. Before World War II a civil war had broken out in that country with two groups fighting for control. During World War II they joined forces to fight their common enemy, Japan, but once the war ended they went back to fighting each other, with the communists eventually winning.

War Events At the end of World War II, Korea was divided in two at latitude 38 degrees north (also known as the 38th parallel) with the intention of bringing the two together. Promised free elections were never allowed, and in 1950 Kim Il Sung, the leader of North Korea, sent his powerful army into South Korea. The United Nations responded quickly, imposing military sanctions. The United States and 19 other nations committed troops to this "police action." Despite initial heavy losses, the combined UN forces finally began to win. Then the situation changed when General Douglas MacArthur, the commander of UN troops in Korea, disobeyed orders to stay in South Korea. Going beyond the 38th parallel into North Korea brought communist China's well-trained and well-equipped army into the war. When the fighting finally ended in 1953, no one was truly victorious. The 38th parallel dividing line remained intact.

Home Front Back on the home front, the American people worried that communism would take over the United States and dominate the world. Senator Joseph McCarthy spearheaded a communist hunt fueled by these fears throughout the country. His television appearances infected the nation with an anti-communist hysteria that ruined numerous lives from politicians to actors and writers. For more on McCarthy read page 17.

Research Topics

Choose one of the following topics to research further. Share your findings with a partner. Explain what the UN and U.S. proved by waging the Korean War.

- Tell how the war might have been different if MacArthur had not invaded North Korea.
- Describe President Truman's policy of containment.
- Detail how the Korean War led to the failure of Democrats to win the 1952 election.

Chronology of the Korean War

Make a transparency of this page for use with the overhead projector. With the class discuss the progression of the Korean War. Have students find the boldfaced locations on a map of Korea. Let the students choose a topic from the chronology to study in depth and have them prepare a short report on their chosen topic.

1950

June 25	**North Korea** invades South Korea.
June 27	UN Security Council asks members to assist **South Korea**.
June 30	Truman orders U.S. ground troops to South Korea.
July 7	General Douglas MacArthur is appointed head of UN command.
Sept. 15	Allied troops stage **Inchon** landing behind enemy lines.
Sept. 26	General MacArthur announces the capture of **Seoul**.
Oct. 7	U.S. troops cross the **38th parallel**.
Oct. 14	**China** moves south into North Korea.
Oct. 19	Allies capture **Pyongyang**.
Oct. 27	Chinese soldiers attack UN troops.
Nov. 26	Allied troops retreat.

1951

Jan. 4	Communist troops occupy Seoul.
Jan. 11	The UN proposes a cease-fire agreement.
Jan. 17	The proposal is rejected by Chinese.
Feb. 1	UN declares China to be an aggressor state.
Mar. 14	Allied troops reoccupy Seoul.
Apr. 11	General MacArthur is fired by President Truman and replaced with General Ridgeway.
June 23	Soviets call for a ceasefire.
July 10	Armistice negotiations begin at **Kaesong**.
Nov. 26	The demarcation line is established.

1952

May 7	A stalemate occurs in the peace talks over POW issues.
Oct. 8	Peace talks are broken off.

1953

Feb. 22	A proposal is made to exchange sick and wounded.
Apr. 20	Sick and wounded are exchanged under Operation Little Switch.
Apr. 26	An armistice talks resume at **Panmunjom**.
July 27	Armistice agreement is signed; the fighting ends.
Aug. 5	Prisoners of war are exchanged under Operation Big Switch.

Mapping Korea

Read about the Korean War on pages 25 and 26. Label the map of Korea below.

China

North Korea

South Korea

USSR

The Sea of Japan

The Yellow Sea

Make a star and label North Korea's capital of Pyongyang.

Make a star and label South Korea's capital of Seoul.

Use a green-colored pencil to draw the 38th Parallel.

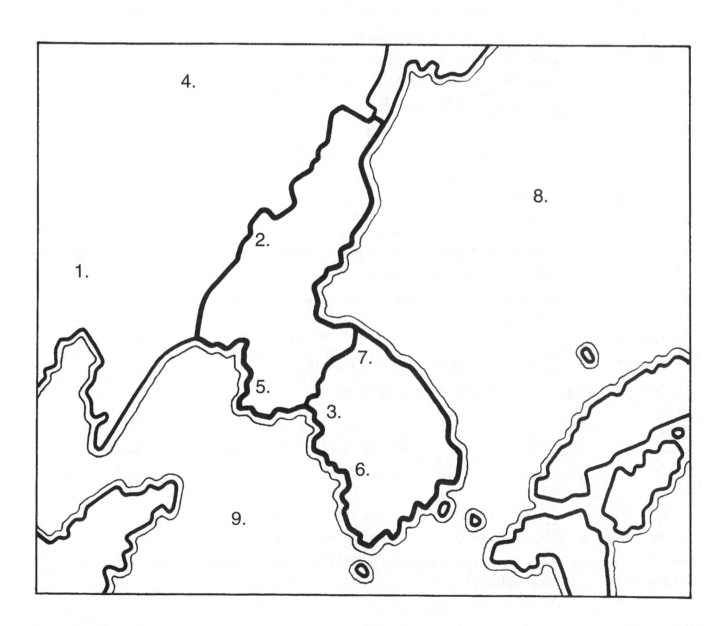

General Douglas MacArthur

During World War II he was the general in command of American forces in the Pacific, and during the Korean War he was appointed chief of the United Nations Command. General Douglas MacArthur was a controversial figure.

Douglas MacArthur was born on January 26, 1880, in Little Rock, Arkansas. His family had a long tradition of military service, and he was no exception, graduating from both the West Texas Military Academy and the United States Military Academy at West Point. In 1908 he graduated from an engineering school and five years later joined the general staff of the War Department.

Douglas MacArthur

His military career began during World War I when he was appointed chief of staff of the 42nd Infantry Division which was sent to France. After distinguishing himself in the war, he returned home to become superintendent of West Point. In 1930 President Hoover appointed him army chief of staff, and two years later he was involved in the unpopular eviction of the Bonus March protestors. Under President Franklin Roosevelt, MacArthur became military adviser to the Philippines and soon was in command of their army. But in 1941 he was forced to retreat when the Japanese invaded the Philippines. "I shall return," he vowed. He was later able to make good on his promise near the end of World War II.

After being appointed supreme commander of the Allied forces, MacArthur was a virtual dictator of Japan throughout the American occupation from 1945–1949. He arranged for food for the Japanese whose cities were in ruins, and he rid the government of militarists. In addition, he arranged for free elections and civil liberties for Japanese citizens. When he left his command, Japan had evolved from a wartime military dictatorship to a postwar democracy.

MacArthur's next foray into battle was in 1950 as chief of the United Nations Command in the Korean War. After a brilliant counterattack, the communists had been driven back into North Korea, close to the Chinese border. The Chinese, however, sent a huge force of soldiers to drive MacArthur back. From there, neither side made much progress. President Truman wanted to negotiate a peace treaty while MacArthur wanted to expand the war and publicly disagreed with the President. MacArthur was fired from his position. Nevertheless, he returned to the U.S. as a hero. Douglas MacArthur died on April 5, 1964.

Suggested Activities

Debate In two groups, debate the question of whether or not President Truman should have fired MacArthur.

Speculation Discuss what might have happened if MacArthur had been allowed to take on the Chinese in the Korean War. What would have been some possible outcomes?

Research Research the Inchon landing and find out why it is considered one of the most brilliant plans in warfare history.

A Visit to Korea

While you are studying about the Korean War you may want to explore the people and culture of Korea itself. Here are some sample activities for you to choose from and try with your class.

Literature Read aloud *The Korean Cinderella* by Shirley Climo (HarperCollins, 1993). Compare it with the Disney version of the same tale. What elements are the same? Which are different? Assign students to read another Korean fairy tale such as *The Princess and the Beggar* by Anne Sibley O'Brien (Scholastic, Inc., 1993).

Holidays Explore some of the traditional Korean holidays such as *Dano* (the Spring Festival) or *Sul* (New Year's Day). Ask students to find out how the Korean events are celebrated, what foods are served, and what time of year each occurs. Compare *Ch'usko*, the Korean Thanksgiving, with a traditional American Thanksgiving.

Dress Pair the students and have them research traditional Korean dress. Direct them to draw pictures of Korean clothing.

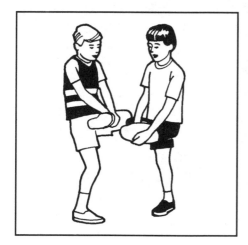

Food Cook some rice with the class; let students eat it with chopsticks. Sample some other Korean foods such as kimchi (available at Korean specialty markets or some larger food stores).

Games Play *Tak Ssaum*, a traditional Korean wrestling game. Carefully pair student volunteers (both should be about the same height and weight). Go outside on a grassy lawn or use a large exercise mat indoors. Opponents stand on one leg and bend the other leg in front of them (see diagram). Tell them to hold on to the ankle with the opposite hand. At a given signal the two contestants bump into each other until one of them loses balance and puts a leg down or falls. No head-bumping is allowed.

Yout is Korea's most popular game. Research and learn how it is played.

Writing Give students a copy of the Korean words below. Instruct them to practice drawing the words and letters.

English	Phonetic Pronuciation	Korean
hello/goodbye	*ahn-nyong*	안녕
mother	*omoni*	어머니
house	*aboji*	아버지
school	*hakkyo*	학교
father	*chip*	집
friend	*ch'in'gn*	친구

Reference

Look What We've Brought You From Korea by Phyllis Shalant (Julian Messner, 1995)

The TV Generation

Children born in the late 1940s were the first generation to grow up with television. The full impact of this phenomenon would not be seen for many years. On this page you will read about the beginnings of television.

History During the late 1940s some television programs debuted, but they reached relatively small audiences. In 1948, there were fewer than 17,000 TV sets in the whole United States. By the end of the 1950s Americans owned an estimated 50 million sets.

Criticisms Criticism of the new industry came quickly. Some called the TV an "idiot box" or the "boob tube," claiming that many programs had little value. Educators were concerned about the impact of TV on their students and worried that students might skip their homework to watch shows. The amount of violence and sex depicted in some programs was also worrisome to many.

Lifestyle Changes Almost overnight the lifestyles of millions of Americans changed as people stayed up later to watch shows. Some people stayed inside their homes more, leaving their houses infrequently. With the invention of the TV dinner in 1954, some families even began eating in front of the television set.

Impact One important impact of television was the business of TV commercials, which brought in over 1.5 billion dollars in advertising money in the early 1950s. Another way television impacted America was in the coast-to-coast programs which allowed people to view firsthand historical events such as political conventions and presidential inaugurations.

A Scandal Quiz shows were popular during the 50s, but *Twenty-One* created the scandal of the decade. Players answered questions, and if they were correct they could choose to keep going. As the questions grew more and more difficult, the prize money grew larger. One contestant, college instructor Charles Van Doren, amassed $129,000 in prize money. In 1958, however, a Congressional investigation revealed that the show was fraudulent and had given questions to Van Doren and others in advance.

Suggested Activities

Movie View the 1995 movie *Quiz Show* for an indepth look at the quiz show scandal of the fifties.

Response What problems facing television viewers are the same today as they were in the 50s?

Debate Choose two groups to debate this question: Who should be responsible for censoring TV programming, individuals (parents) or the government?

Contrast Contrast the current criticisms of TV viewing with criticisms of TV viewing in the fifties.

Survey Keep a survey of your own or your families' television viewing for one week. Tally the results and compare and discuss them with the whole class.

TV in the Fifties

You may already be familiar with some of the fifties television programs because they can be seen in syndication on cable channels or may still be on the air (*The Price Is Right*, for example). Below is a list of some of the most popular shows on TV during the fifties followed by a comparison project for you to complete.

What's My Line? John Daly hosted this show for its 17-year run. A celebrity panel tried to guess the occupation of various guests.

The Ed Sullivan Show One of the biggest names in television was Ed Sullivan. In his weekly variety show Sullivan showcased all types of entertainers from acrobats to comics to opera signers. Many performers, including Elvis Presley and the Beatles, were introduced to the nation on this program.

Milton Berle Known as "Mr. Television," Milton Berle was another big name on TV. For five years his comedy show was rated number one among all the networks.

I Love Lucy Husband and wife comedy team Desi Arnaz and Lucille Ball starred in this zany comedy. Perhaps the most popular television show of the decade, the program attracted 50 million viewers weekly. Look for it today in syndication. Another popular husband and wife team, George Burns and Gracie Allen, hosted a popular weekly series from 1950 to 1958. See page 44 for more on this duo.

Westerns The western was a popular format in the fifties. Four of the top series were *Gunsmoke*, *Wagon Train*, *Have Gun Will Travel*, and *Wyatt Earp*. Among the younger crowd, *Hopalong Cassidy* and *Roy Rogers* were both well-received westerns.

Dragnet Jack Webb starred in this police drama. Its star and style would later be parodied in many TV shows and movies.

American Bandstand This Philadelphia-based teen dance program which featured celebrity guests and teenagers dancing the latest steps to the popular tunes of the day was first broadcast nationally in 1958, with a new host—the forever-young Dick Clark.

Children's Programming Some shows were developed especially for the young audience, including the following: *Captain Kangaroo* lasted until the late 1980s; *Lassie* was about a boy and his faithful dog; *Kukla, Fran and Ollie* featured Fran and her two silly puppet friends; *Howdy Doody* starred Buffalo Bob and a host of characters including Clarabelle the Clown, Mr. Flubadub, and Princess Summer Fall Winter Spring; and *The Mickey Mouse Club*, whose most popular mouseketeer, Annette Funicello, became a star actress and singer.

Fifties Families The typical fifties family was portrayed in a number of long-running series, including *The Ozzie and Harriet Show* which featured the real-life Nelson family; son Ricky was also a singing star and teen idol. *Father Knows Best* and *Leave It to Beaver* also portrayed strong family units with stay-at-home moms, well-mannered children, and benevolent fathers.

Suggested Activity

Compare the way families are depicted today to the way families were portrayed in the fifties. Construct a Venn diagram to show the similarities and differences between TV in the 1950s and TV today.

A TV Questionnaire

Fill out this questionnaire about your television viewing habits. Use your answers to contribute to class discussions. Remember, there are no right or wrong answers. Note that some questions require more than one response.

1. The number of hours I currently spend watching TV per week is
   a. 0–5   b. 6–10   c. 11–15   d. 16 or more

2. Some of the reasons I watch TV are (circle all that apply)
   a. boredom   b. educational value   c. stress relief   d. entertainment

3. Type of programs I like to watch include (circle all that apply)
   a. dramas   d. old movies   g. educational shows
   b. talk shows   e. soaps   h. sports
   c. cartoons   f. news and weather   i. other_____

4. Rank the above types of programs in order of preference from most-to-least liked (use the letters).
   1. _____   4. _____   7. _____
   2. _____   5. _____   8. _____
   3. _____   6. _____   9. _____

5. Name your three all-time favorite regularly-scheduled TV programs.
   1. _____   2. _____   3. _____

6. Circle the ways in which TV influences your life.
   a. your choice of clothing   e. how you treat others
   b. your behavior towards your parents and teachers   f. the way you view yourself
   g. things you do
   c. the things you say   h. what you eat
   d. products you buy

7. Read each choice below and circle the one you would rather do in each case.
   a. exercise or watch TV   d. engage in a hobby or watch TV
   b. read a newspaper or watch TV   e. read a book or watch TV
   c. work on a computer or watch TV   f. do homework or watch TV
   g. talk with a friend or watch TV

8. Rate the importance of TV in your life.

   10   9   8   7   6   5   4   3   2   1
   very important   somewhat important   not important

9. How would your life be different without television?

   _____

   _____

   _____

Droodles

In the early 1950s the *Garry Moore Show* was a popular weekly television variety program. During one evening's shows in 1953, gag writer Roger Price persuaded host Garry Moore to show the audience some sketches which he called *Droodles* (see samples below). They were well received, and by the end of the following week Price had received 15,000 fan letters.

Over the next two years Price published three books of his *Droodles*. Look at the sample *Droodles* below. Draw and title five of your own *Droodles* in the boxes provided.

the Washington Monument as seen by an English sheep dog	the Invisible Man with a speck in his eye
zebra in a snowstorm	

The Fifties Woman

During World War II American women participated in the war effort at home and abroad by working in factories, volunteering, and serving in the armed services as nurses, secretaries, and even pilots. For the first time women found out that they were capable of doing jobs traditionally reserved for men. Once the servicemen returned home from war, however, women workers were quickly replaced by former G.I.s. Life returned to the pre-war pattern in which most women did not work outside the home. After the war, couples began marrying in record numbers and produced a baby boom of an unparalleled number of births. The demand for affordable housing rose dramatically. As part of the G.I. Bill, servicemen were entitled to special inexpensive housing loans. To meet the need, mass-produced suburban communities, based on a New York project called Levittown, were built across the country, and families filled them up quickly. The ideal suburban family consisted of a mother, father, two children, and a dog. A station wagon was the car of choice, and everyone was white, young, and earned approximately the same income. Mothers were expected to stay at home, taking care of their husbands' and families' needs. For some, however, the traditional roles began to change in the suburbs. Some husbands did the grocery shopping, and some wives painted and did other maintenance chores. Although some women found the suburban lifestyle boring, they were not ready to speak out about it. That would come with the sixties when women openly fought for equal rights.

Although most women accepted this stereotyped image and style of living, there were some who rebelled against society and joined the ranks of the Beatniks. Originally a West Coast group centered in both San Francisco and Los Angeles, Beatniks also had followers in New York City. Beatniks created their own vocabulary (chicks for girls, pads for apartments, etc.), experimented with marijuana, and lived in sparsely furnished apartments. They especially liked the jazz music of Thelonius Monk and Miles Davis and protest songs, blues, and Depression ballads. A female Beatnik wore black leotards, no lipstick, and dark eyeshadow. It was a perfect match for the men who favored beards, short hair, khaki pants, sweaters, and sandals. Although the Beatnik movement frightened most Americans, they were also fascinated by this alternative lifestyle. In the sixties many would choose to rebel against society.

Suggested Activities

Discussion How women's role in society changed and yet stayed the same since the 1950s? Discuss your views of women in society and what influences your view the most (religious upbringing, parents' views, etc.)?

Beatnik Day Dress as Beatniks for a day. Use the Beat language (for more words and phrases, see page 93 of this book), listen to Beat music, and recite poetry. Applaud performances by snapping fingers.

A Woman's Place

Say the name Margaret Chase Smith, and at least one image comes to mind: a trademark single red rose pinned to her clothing. This former U.S. Representative and Senator left an indelible mark on American politics and proved that a woman's place is in the House . . . and in the Senate.

Margaret Chase was born in Skowhegan, Maine, on December 14, 1897. She grew up with her two sisters and one brother in a white frame house which stood next door to her father's barber shop.

Margaret Chase Smith

After Chase graduated from high school in 1916, she taught school for a short time in a one-room schoolhouse. Through the years she worked at a variety of jobs until she married Clyde Smith, a local political and business leader, in May of 1930. When Clyde was elected to the U.S. House of Representatives in 1936, Margaret accompanied him to Washington, D.C. In addition to acting as his secretary, she helped write his speeches and conducted research on upcoming legislation. A heart attack kept Smith from running for reelection in 1940, and Margaret agreed to be a temporary candidate until her husband's health improved. Unfortunately, Clyde died after suffering another heart attack. Margaret was then chosen to serve out the remainder of his term.

An enthusiastic worker, Margaret accepted assignments to a variety of committees, always with an eye out for the interests of her home state and women's issues. When a seat in the Senate was being vacated in 1947, Margaret took a risk and went after that Senate seat. Her subsequent win caused quite a stir and gave her the distinction of being the first woman to have served in both the Senate and the House of Representatives.

For the most part, Margaret kept a low profile, but when another senator, Joseph McCarthy, began making unfounded accusations, she stood up to him. In her "Declaration of Conscience" speech she spoke out against McCarthy and warned against the use of the Senate as a forum for character assassination. McCarthy responded by ridiculing Smith and replacing her on an important Senate subcommittee.

After her third term, Senator Smith announced her candidacy for the Republican presidential nomination. Despite her excellent qualifications and a valiant effort, she lost to another senator, Barry Goldwater of Arizona. Smith continued in the Senate until 1972. On July 6, 1989, she was honored with the Presidential Medal of Freedom, the nation's highest civilian honor.

Suggested Activities

Discussion Discuss the differences between Senators and Representatives: their qualifications, duties, and lengths of their terms.

Others Research and list all the women who currently hold seats in Congress.

Resource An excellent resource for this page is *Women of the U.S. Congress* by Isobel V. Morin (The Oliver Press, Inc., 1994).

The Billy Graham Crusades

He has been called the greatest evangelist of the 20th century. Since the 1940s he has brought the word of God to people all over the globe. His goals in life were to bring God's message to as many people as possible and to build peace and friendship among all peoples. Meet the man behind these lofty ideals: Reverend Billy Graham.

Billy Graham

William Franklin Graham, later called Billy, was born on November 7, 1918, on a farm near Charlotte, North Carolina. As children, he and his brother helped their father with the chores on the farm. Every morning at three o'clock they were up to milk the cows, and after school there were more chores. It is no wonder, then, that Graham had trouble staying awake in class. A poor pupil, he consoled himself with the thought that he did not need to study because he was going to be a farmer. Trouble followed him into high school where he got into fights and skipped classes.

In his senior year, Graham's life changed when he heard evangelist Mordacai Ham speak. Deeply moved by the preacher's words, Graham dropped his wild ways and in the fall entered college. While attending the Florida Bible Institute in Tampa, Graham knew that God was calling him to preach. His thick accent stood in his way, however, so he practiced and practiced until he was taken seriously. In 1939 Graham became a Baptist and a minister.

After graduating from the Bible Institute, Reverend Billy Graham attended Wheaton College in Illinois where he met his future wife, Ruth Bell. Following a two-year courtship, the couple was married. Graham became a pastor and was asked to take over a radio program called *Songs in the Night*. The broadcast was such a hit with listeners that Graham was asked to try something else. The result was a Youth for Christ rally aimed at World War II servicemen. This movement quickly spread to other cities across the U.S. and even into Europe. In 1949 Billy Graham held a crusade in a tent in Los Angeles. Graham's fame grew, and he received invitations to preach all over the world.

During the fifties, Graham conducted crusades all across America, but it was not until 1958 that he returned to his hometown of Charlotte. He had previously refused to hold a crusade in which blacks and whites could not worship together. As he walked out into the crowd opening night, he saw more than 14,000 people, black and white, all waiting to hear his words. Billy Graham continued to bring his spiritual guidance to people well into the 1990s.

Suggested Activities

Discussion Discuss the sights and sounds of a crusade held in a tent. What might you expect to see and hear at one of Graham's crusades?

Presidents Research Graham's relationship with Presidents Eisenhower and Nixon.

An Extraordinary Bus Ride

She has been called the mother of the civil rights movement, but Rosa McCauley Parks does not consider herself to be extraordinary. Born on February 4, 1915, in Tuskegee, Alabama, McCauley had a normal childhood. She grew up on a farm and attended an all-black school in her neighborhood. Her high school education was cut short by her mother's death, but she finished her schooling after her marriage to Raymond Parks. In 1943 she joined the NAACP (National Association for the Advancement of Colored People) and worked with the Voters' League, registering African Americans to vote. Then came the fateful day.

Rosa McCauley Parks

The bus ride on December 1, 1955, began as usual. After completing her job as a seamstress for a Montgomery department store, Parks boarded the bus to go home. As was required, she took a seat in the back of the bus. When all the seats filled up, Parks was asked to vacate hers for a white man who was just getting on the bus. (At that time in Montgomery the law required blacks to sit at the back of the bus and to give up their seats for white people when all other seats were filled.) On this day, however, Parks refused to move. The bus driver stopped the bus and called for policemen who whisked her away to jail. NAACP leader Edgar Daniel Nixon posted her bail and determined that Rosa Parks would be the last African American arrested for such an action.

Along with other black leaders, including Dr. Martin Luther King, Jr., Nixon declared a one-day boycott of all city buses. Leaflets announcing the boycott were distributed throughout the city, and on the appointed day the results were dramatic. Not one African American rode on any buses there. Because it was such a success, the boycott was extended indefinitely.

For their actions blacks were harassed on the street, hundreds of their leaders were arrested, and many lost their jobs. Still, the boycott continued with African Americans turning to alternative methods of transportation, including walking, carpooling, riding bicycles, and even riding mules. The boycott ended when, after 381 days, the U.S. Supreme Court ruled in favor of Rosa Parks and declared Alabama bus segregation laws unconstitutional. It had cost the bus company $750,000 in lost revenues, but the gains in human dignity were priceless.

Suggested Activity

Role-Play In small groups, write a script for a role-play about Rosa Parks's historic bus ride. Take turns presenting your skits to the rest of the class. For a prepared play, see the book *Take a Walk in Their Shoes* by Glennette Tilley Turner (Puffin Books, 1989).

Making Schools Equal

There was a time in the United States when separate schools for blacks and whites were common, especially in the South, and perfectly legal. The case of *Plessy v. Ferguson* in 1896 had ruled that schools could be separate as long as they were equal. Unfortunately, the equal part was never realized, and conditions in black schools were mostly deplorable. With the case of *Brown v. the Board of Education of Topeka* in 1953, the tide was finally turned in the right direction. Here is a look at the ruling and the events that led up to the case.

When Oliver Brown went to register his daughter Linda at their neighborhood school, he learned it was for whites only. Topeka, Kansas, where they resided, had city laws which set up separate schools for blacks and whites. Linda would have to walk six blocks through heavy traffic before reaching the bus stop where she would board the school bus for black students. Mr. Brown did not want his daughter subjected to these hazards, particularly when the neighborhood school was a safe seven–block walk from their home. The decision was made to fight the Topeka Board of Education in court. Linda Brown was joined by dozens of other students as plaintiffs.

Thurgood Marshall, senior counsel of the NAACP Legal Defense Fund, directed the case. Much of their argument centered on the interpretation of the 14th Amendment. It was the NAACP's stand that the purpose of the amendment was to put an end to segregation in the area of education. The nine Supreme Court justices heard the arguments, and on May 17, 1954, they announced their decision. In his opinion Chief Justice Earl Warren stated that separate but equal had no place in American education.

Once the decision had been handed down, the justices faced the task of determining how the ruling would be enforced. For a year the debate raged on until the Supreme Court declared that the states had control over how the order would go into effect. Many states dragged their feet and did little about integration until the Civil Rights Act of 1964 was passed.

One district in Little Rock, Arkansas, agreed to begin integration in 1957. The nine black students who tried to enter Central High School were greeted by National Guard troops who prevented them from going into the building. After three weeks, President Eisenhower ordered Army paratroopers to escort the nine to school. Other states continued to stall efforts to enroll black students in white schools, and desegregation moved at a slow pace well into the 1960s.

Suggested Activities

Introduction Read and discuss *The Story of Ruby Bridges* by Robert Coles (Scholastic, Inc., 1995).

Resource For an indepth look at this famous case, read *Brown v. Board of Education* by Harvey Fireside and Sarah Betsy Fuller (Enslow Publishers, Inc., 1994).

A Man of Many Firsts

The title "Man of Many Firsts" is an appropriate one for Ralph J. Bunche. On the personal side, he was the first member of his family to finish college. The first African American to earn an advanced degree in political science from Harvard University and the first black to win the Nobel Peace Prize, he proved to be an inspiration and role model for his race. Read on for more about this important politician.

Ralph J. Bunche was born on August 7, 1904, into a poor household which included his parents, aunts, uncle, and grandmother. It was a happy, loving family, and the young Bunche grew up believing in himself. When he was eleven years old, the family moved from Detroit, Michigan, to New Mexico. In school his favorite teacher was Miss Sweet because she taught about the different countries around the world. Bunche was eager to visit these places and to learn more about them.

Ralph J. Bunche

After his parents died, Bunche's grandmother moved the family to Los Angeles, California. The only African American in his class, he earned the highest grades and graduated from his high school with honors. With his outstanding academic record, he was easily admitted to UCLA. In addition to his studies, Bunche played basketball, baseball, and football for UCLA. Although he graduated with honors, a lack of money stood in the way of his dreams of attending Harvard Law School. Fortunately, a women's club in the area raised the money to help him pay for tuition. In 1928 he completed his studies in government and taught at Howard University in Washington, D.C. Two years later he married schoolteacher Ruth Harris. For two years Bunche studied the African people and subsequently earned a Ph.D. in political science.

During World War II Bunche was asked to work for the State Department, and he helped to found the United Nations. His first important negotiating job came during the 1948 war between the Arabs and Israelis. Much to his and the world's relief, a peace treaty was finally signed. In 1950 he was awarded the Nobel Peace Prize for his efforts in ending the war in the Holy Land. Ralph Bunche was the first African American to win this honor. For 25 years Bunche worked for the UN. Poor health forced him to leave in 1971, and only six months later, on December 7, 1971, he died. The world had lost an invaluable resource.

Suggested Activities

United Nations Define the United Nations and its peace-keeping role. How successful has it been in this respect in recent years?

Holy War Find out the causes of the 1948 Holy War. Has a permanent peace been made there?

Peace Prize Ralph Bunche is in fine company with other Nobel prize winners. Find out the names of others who won the coveted peace prize during the 1950s.

Discussion Discuss some of the adversities that Ralph Bunche faced during his school years and how he overcame them.

Asian Pacific American Spotlight

A number of Asian Pacific Americans have made significant contributions to society. Some were born in the United States while others were immigrants to America. Some of the figures featured on this page were born in the fifties while others made their mark in history during that decade. The following Asian Pacific Americans represent a variety of careers and a vast array of accomplishments. Read about each one and do further research on the person who interests you most.

Yo Yo Ma, Cellist
Heritage: Chinese
Facts: Born in 1955 in Paris, France, he moved to America with his family in 1962. At the age of five he gave his first public concert. Today, he is in demand as a soloist and a recording artist.

Daniel K. Inouye, Congressman
Heritage: Japanese
Facts: As a soldier during World War II, this Hawaiian native lost his right arm. When Hawaii became a state in 1959, he became the state's first United States Representative and the first Japanese American to serve in Congress.

Dong Kingman, Artist
Heritage: Chinese
Facts: Born in 1911 in Oakland, California, he studied both Oriental and Western art. During the 1950s he traveled to Asia as a cultural envoy for the State Department. Some of his paintings have appeared in films including *The Flower Drum Song*.

Sammy Lee, Athlete, Physician, Coach
Heritage: Korean
Facts: During the 1948 Summer Olympics in London, England, he won a gold medal in platform diving. Four years later in Helsinki he repeated the feat to become the first person to win back-to-back Olympic gold medals in diving.

Hiram Fong, Attorney
Heritage: Chinese
Facts: A native Hawaiian, Fong graduated from Harvard and founded Honolulu's first multicultural law firm. In 1950 he became vice-president of the territorial Constitutional Convention and helped bring Hawaii to statehood in 1959.

Amy Tan, Writer
Heritage: Chinese
Facts: Amy Tan was born in 1953 and never knew about her heritage until her father died. After her mother revealed some family secrets, Amy wrote novels based on these incidents. *The Joy Luck Club* was just one of her best-selling novels.

Carlos Bulosan, Poet
Heritage: Filipino
Facts: When Bulosan immigrated to California in the mid-1930s, there were state laws discriminating against Filipinos. After supporting labor movements to help Filipinos, he began to write poetry. His best-known work is *American Is in the Heart*.

Reference
Extraordinary Asian Pacific Americans by Susan Sinnott (Childrens Press, 1993).

Revelations

On January 5, 1931, Alvin Ailey, Jr., was born to Alvin and Lula Elizabeth Ailey. The overcrowded household was already home to Alvin's parents, a grandfather, an aunt and uncle, and eight cousins. When Alvin Ailey was only six months old, his father left. To support her son, Lula Ailey worked at a number of odd jobs. In 1942 she found a high-paying job in an aircraft factory, and she and her son moved to California. It was a good move for young Ailey because he was exposed to concert dance for the first time. Not only did he attend a ballet with his high school class but he later saw performances of the Katherine Dunham Dance Company, an all-black dance troupe. Some years would pass, though, before Ailey would head his own dance troupe.

Alvin Ailey, Jr.

While Ailey attended college at UCLA, he also trained with the Lester Horton Dance Theater in Hollywood. When Horton died suddenly, Ailey took over for awhile as artistic director of the company. A turning point in his career came when he was asked to dance in the Broadway show *House of Flowers*. It featured a number of prominent African American dancers and was a success with its sensuous, energetic dances. Afterwards, Ailey decided to stay in New York City, where he continued to study dance and theater under prominent choreographers and acting teachers. Over the years he won a number of acting roles and some directing assignments.

In 1958 Ailey got his real start on what was to be a 30-year career when he directed and performed at the 92nd Street Y. Because government money was not available to the arts at that time, Ailey and his group constructed their own costumes from old curtains and other found items. Dancers carried their own costumes and props from rehearsal hall to rehearsal hall. It was time to establish a permanent company. Glowing reviews of Ailey's dance routines, particularly one called Revelations, helped the group find a permanent residence in 1960.

In 1962 Alvin Ailey's American Dance Theater was chosen by President Kennedy to be part of an international cultural program. The group traveled abroad throughout Asia, Australia, South America, and Europe. Ailey continued to bring his unique dance style to audiences until his death on December 1, 1989.

Suggested Activities

Biography For more information about Alvin Ailey, Jr., read the biography *Alvin Ailey, Jr.: A Life in Dance* by Julinda Lewis-Ferguson (Walker and Company, 1994).

Influences Katherine Dunham was influential in Alvin Ailey's career. Find out some facts about her life and write a one-page report.

Rebels and the Movies

Teenagers have a culture all their own. They dress differently from adults, listen to their own music, invent slang words to express themselves, and start new fads. Often, teenagers feel misunderstood by older generations, and they rebel against authority figures (parents, teachers, the government). Ever since the 1950s, movies have tried to capture this teen rebellion. On this page you will find summaries to three important youth rebellion movies of the fifties.

The Wild One

This 1954 film is based on a true story and stars Marlon Brando and Lee Marvin. The plot centers around the conflict between the small town of Wrightsville and an outlaw biker gang called the Black Rebels. The bikers quickly disrupt the usual quiet of the town. Johnny, the leader of the gang, is drawn to Kathie, a bar owner's niece, and they become uneasy friends. When Johnny gets into trouble with the law, Kathie testifies on his behalf. He is released and rides out of town alone.

Marlon Brando

Activity Compare this film with the 1969 movie *Easy Rider* starring Jack Nicholson and Peter Fonda. Which is more believable or realistic?

The Blackboard Jungle

A 1955 film, *The Blackboard Jungle* stars Glenn Ford, Vic Morrow, and Sidney Poitier and shows the problems of racism and poverty in schools. The story is really about how these factors affect students and their attitude toward school. Teacher Richard Dadier (Ford) is just out of college. He wants to do something about the students' problems, but they resist and disrespect his efforts. Even the other teachers at the school laugh at Dadier for trying; they have already given up. But Dadier is a fighter, and despite some misunderstandings and physical confrontations with some students, he finally seems to be reaching his class by the end of the film.

Activity In 1967 Sidney Poitier starred as a teacher in working-class London in *To Sir with Love*. What issues were the same in both films? How else are the two films similar?

Rebel Without a Cause

This film was also released in 1955, but it shows that teens from nice homes can also be rebellious. Starring James Dean, Natalie Wood, and Sal Mineo, the story is about suburban teens who are having problems with their parents. James Dean's character has a hard time fitting in. The situation is made even more unbearable with his parents' constant fighting. Other characters have parents who are distant and unavailable for them. The movie is a realistic portrayal and displays an acute understanding of teens.

Activity James Dean's performance in *Rebel Without a Cause* helped change the way teenagers were portrayed in films. Learn more about this legend, his other films, and how and when he died.

Reference

Youth Rebellion Movies by Marc Perlman (Lerner Publications Company, 1993).

The Magic Kingdom

While watching his daughters play on the merry-go-round at a local park, Walt Disney wondered why there was not a place where children and parents could play at the same time. He toyed with the idea of building a small amusement park across the street from his studio, but the plans were only dreams. It was a dream Disney never forgot, and in the early 1950s he began preparations for a family park. The result was Disneyland, 180 acres of fun and entertainment in Anaheim, California. Billed as the "happiest place on earth," it has undergone numerous changes since it first opened in 1955 and remains a favorite family vacation destination.

For an inside look at the beginnings of Disneyland, unscramble the letter groups in the box below. Then write the words correctly on the corresponding lines.

1. ncale	4. leykwe	7. urevbodla	10. lsphata	13. cseuscs
2. pakdlsre	5. solan	8. texcoi	11. lodofed	14. ensev
3. crtepjo	6. uaylto	9. streadsi	12. eclatste	15. stviroi

On a trip to Copenhagen, Denmark, Walt Disney was impressed by the Tivoli Gardens because they were so 1. _____ and guests were treated well. He vowed to build a park that 2. _____ like that. To finance the 3. _____ Walt borrowed money from employees, sold his vacation house, and cleaned out his own savings. When that was not enough, Walt launched a 4. _____ television series. ABC put up $500,000 in cash and agreed to guarantee $4.5 million more in 5. _____ . The 6. _____ of Disneyland differed from the traditional amusement parks. Instead of one long 7. _____ , Main Street led to a hub which led to other themed areas. The most difficult ride to create was the Jungle Cruise with its animals and 8. _____ vegetation.

Opening day proved to be a 9. _____ . There were not enough trash cans, and the heat of the day melted the 10. _____ . Rides broke down, the *Mark Twain's* lower deck 11. _____ , and there were not enough restrooms for all the people. Even the live 12. _____ had problems—microphones went dead, and cameras caught Walt Disney off guard. Despite these problems the park met with extraordinary 13. _____ . Only 14. _____ weeks after opening its doors, the one-millionth 15. _____ entered through the gates of the Magic Kingdom.

Burns and Allen

One of the most popular series on television during the 1950s was the comedy program *The George Burns and Gracie Allen Show.* It starred real-life couple George Burns and Gracie Allen, and ran from 1950 to 1958 when Allen retired. Although Gracie Allen died six years later, George Burns continued with his show business career almost until his 100th birthday. Read on for some more information about this beloved comedy duo.

George Burns and Gracie Allen

George Burns was born Nathan Birnbaum in New York City on January 20, 1896. Gracie Allen was born in San Francisco on July 20, 1906. Together they became one of the finest husband-and-wife comedy acts in American show business. Burns' career started in vaudeville when he was only seven years old. In 1922 Burns was appearing as one half of a male comedy team when a friend introduced him to Gracie Ethel Cecile Rosalie Allen, a 17-year-old secretarial school student. She, too, had show business ties—she was just three when she first performed in her father's act. Burns persuaded Allen to join him in a new comedy act. It would be her job to feed him the straight lines and he would deliver the gags, but it did not stay that way for long. When Allen's character got most of the laughs, Burns quickly rewrote the act and made himself the straight man and Allen the comedian.

When Burns and Allen married in 1926, they had already made it to the Palace Theater on Broadway, the biggest thing in vaudeville. Radio was becoming the new star machine, and Burns and Allen were just right for the nonvisual medium. For 18 years the couple had a program on the air, one of the most popular shows of its time. In 1950 a new opportunity came in the form of television. *The George Burns and Gracie Allen Show* featured an initial stand-up comedic segment with George Burns and characters who portrayed themselves.

In 1958 Allen announced her retirement; recurring heart problems made it too difficult for her to work. On August 27, 1964, she suffered a fatal heart attack.

The grief-stricken Burns went back to work playing clubs and making movies. At 79, his work in the film *The Sunshine Boys* won him an Academy Award for Best Supporting Actor. His biggest movie role, though, was as the Supreme Being in the film *Oh, God!* and its two sequels. Around this same time he began writing the first of his many books. George Burns died in 1996 at the age of 100. He had explored every medium available from vaudeville to television and had succeeded in all of them.

Suggested Activities

Comparisons Watch an episode of *The George Burns and Gracie Allen Show* (available on video from Columbia Tri-Star Home Entertainment). Compare it to the popular nineties sitcom *Seinfeld*.

Vaudeville Research vaudeville—what it was, where it started, some of its famous performers, and what became of it.

Fifties Sports Highlights

This page provides an overview of sports during the fifties and highlights some important people and events of the decade.

Baseball In 1951 the New York Giants made the greatest comeback in major league history when they captured the National League pennant. The Giants and Dodgers made history by leaving New York City and moving to the West Coast to become the San Francisco Giants and the Los Angeles Dodgers. By far, the best baseball team of the fifties was the New York Yankees managed by Casey Stengel. In 1956 their pitcher, Don Larsen, pitched the only no-hit, no-run game in world series history.

Boxing In 1951 Rocky Marciano defeated former heavyweight champ Joe Louis. Marciano reigned as heavyweight champion from 1952 to 1956.

Football The Cleveland Browns remained the dominant football team throughout the decade with African American Jim Brown the greatest football runner of the times. One televised game in 1958 is credited with turning millions of Americans into fans of professional football. Johnny Unitas' short passes and runs helped the Colts beat the New York Giants in a "sudden death" overtime play.

Track and Field On May 6, 1954, Roger Bannister of England became the first man in history to run the mile in under four minutes. American Parry O'Brien broke a record in the shot put when he tossed an iron ball more than 60 feet (18.3 m). A new world mark in the high jump was set when Californian Charles Dumas cleared the bar at 7' ½" (2.28 m).

Basketball Two teams remained standouts during the fifties, the Minneapolis Lakers and the Boston Celtics. African American player Bill Russell was a superstar on the Celtics team.

Tennis Maureen "Little Mo" Connolly won the National Women's Singles Championship at age 16, the youngest national champion since 1901. Althea Gibson became the first black invited to compete in the United States Lawn Tennis Association's National Championships. (See page 46 for more on Gibson.) Pancho Gonzales was the outstanding male tennis player of the fifties.

Golf Badly injured in a near-fatal car crash, golfer Ben Hogan returned to the greens 17 months later to win the United States Open. He went on to win five more major tournament events. In 1950 the Associated Press named Babe Didrikson the most outstanding female athlete of the first half-century. Despite being diagnosed with cancer in 1953, she won the 1954 United States Women's Open and went on to win six more tournaments before her death in 1956.

Suggested Activity

Sports Report Write a sports report about any of the athletes named above. Include the athlete's name, dates of birth and death, facts about his or her childhood, obstacles that the athlete had to overcome in his or her life, and highlights of his or her career.

Althea Gibson

In the 1950s Althea Gibson gained worldwide fame for her athletic ability, but part of the fame can be attributed to her becoming the first African American to be admitted to the U.S. Lawn Association Championships at Forest Hills, New York, in August of 1950.

Gibson was born in Sumpter, South Carolina, but was raised in New York City where she played basketball, shuffleboard, and volleyball. Paddle tennis was another of her favorite sports, and she became so good that she won many local competitions. Her athleticism caught the eye of a local coach, Buddy Walker, who bought Gibson her first tennis racket and introduced her to the game of tennis. Harlem, where she lived, did not have many tennis courts, so Gibson had to practice on handball courts. Despite this disadvantage, Gibson became a good player and in 1950, at age 23, became the first African American to play in the U.S. Open. The following year she broke the race barrier again when she became the first African American to play at Wimbledon in England. Following several years of modest

Althea Gibson

success and many disappointments, Gibson was ready to call it quits, but her coach encouraged her to make a foreign tour. She went on to win 18 tournaments. After winning the 1956 Wimbledon championship, she returned home to Harlem and was greeted with a ticker-tape parade. In 1957 Gibson won the women's singles title at the U.S. Open and the following year repeated her Wimbledon and U.S. Open wins.

Althea Gibson overcame the odds and worked hard to achieve her goals and win major titles. She became an inspiration to all women and paved the way for other African Americans to participate in the game. This former tennis queen was inducted into the National Lawn Tennis Hall of Fame in 1972.

Suggested Activities

Others Discuss some past and current professional African American tennis players including Arthur Ashe, Zina Garrison, MaliVai Washington, and Chanda Rubin. Learn more about them and how they advanced through the ranks.

Court Visit a nearby tennis court and identify the playing lines. Briefly discuss how the game is played and what the lines signify. Your teacher may want to invite the physical education specialist to lecture your class on this topic.

Terms Write some tennis terms on the board and, in small groups, define each one: *net, love, out, side out, advantage, wide, volley, serve.*

Observe Watch a tennis match. Identify various tennis terms, court features, and rules of the game.

Comparisons Compare tennis with racquetball or some other racket sport. Make a Venn diagram to show how the two are alike and different.

Baseball Greats

Four of baseball's greatest hitters of the 1950s are highlighted on this page. Each of these players set and broke amazing records during their careers.

Hank Aaron

Mickey Mantle

Willie Mays

Joe DiMaggio

Hank Aaron

Henry L. "Hank" Aaron, an African American, was born on February 5, 1934, in Mobile, Alabama. At the age of 17 he signed up with a team in a Negro league and in 1954 was drafted by the major league Milwaukee Braves, which moved to Atlanta in 1966. Later in his career he returned to play for the Milwaulkee Brewers. His most memorable baseball moment came when he hit his 715th home run to surpass Babe Ruth's longstanding record. When Aaron retired in 1976 after 23 major league seasons, that home run total had reached 755.

Mickey Mantle

New York Yankee center fielder Mickey Mantle was one of the most-feared power hitters of the 1950s. He led the American League in home runs four times during his eighteen-year career, had ten seasons batting more than .300, four slugging titles, three Most Valuable Player awards, and a lifetime average of .353. He was probably the game's most powerful switch-hitter ever. Mantle was born on October 20, 1931, in Spavinaw, Oklahoma, and died in 1996 after a liver transplant operation.

Willie Mays

Born William Howard Mayes, Jr. on May 6, 1931, in Westfield, Alabama, African American Willie Mays began his professional baseball career with the New York Giants in 1951. Known as the "Say hey kid," this popular batter and centerfielder made the most famous catch in baseball history at the 1954 World Series with his back-to-the plate, over-the-shoulder grab of a 425-foot drive. The Giants moved to San Francisco for the 1958 season. Mayes, always a crowd favorite with New Yorkers, won over the San Francisco fans with his playing ability. Throughout his 22-year career he hit 660 home runs, ending third on the overall home run list just behind Hank Aaron and Babe Ruth.

Joe DiMaggio

Nicknamed "The Yankee Clipper," and "Joltin' Joe," Joe DiMaggio was born on November 25, 1914, in Martinez, California. As a centerfielder for the New York Yankees, he led his team to nine World Series titles. His trademark was his wide stance—the widest of anyone in baseball—which enabled him to earn a lifetime batting average of .325 and a slugging average of .579, making him number six on the all-time list. In 1941 he batted safely in 56 consecutive games. After several injuries, Joe retired in 1952 with 361 career home runs. He went on to marry movie star Marilyn Monroe and became a celebrity television spokesperson.

Suggested Activities

Terms Find out the difference between a hitting average and a slugging average. A complete explanation can be found in the book *Sluggers* by George Sullivan (Macmillan Publishing Company, 1991).

Statistics In small groups, make charts comparing statistics about the four players listed on this page. For example, chart the number of home runs, runs batted in, and triples.

The Battle Against Polio

Once known as infantile paralysis because many of its victims were young children, poliomyelitis, commonly called polio, reached epidemic proportions during the forties and early fifties. In 1952 over 57,000 cases of polio were reported.

Polio is a highly contagious disease of the central nervous system caused by a virus. The majority of cases are nonparalytic and cause only minor symptoms. When the virus enters the central nervous system, it attacks motor neurons, causing paralysis of the arms and legs. In the worst cases, called bulbar polio, the chest muscles become paralyzed.

Polio patients with chest paralysis were placed in Drinker respirators, or "iron lungs." These machines were almost as large as a compact car and exerted a push and pull motion on the chest. Unfortunately, while the use of these machines saved lives, it also contributed to the crippling effects of polio since limbs could not be exercised. This led to contraction and shortening of muscles, adding to the lack of mobility. Elizabeth Kenny, an Australian nurse, pioneered the use of moist heat and physical therapy to treat victims of the crippling virus. Weakened arms and legs required braces.

In an attempt to control the epidemic spread of this disease, public pools and parks were closed, and parents advised their children not to drink from public water fountains. Some communities canceled large public gatherings, including graduations. Families of polio patients faced a period of quarantine. The March of Dimes, founded as the National Foundation for Infantile Paralysis by Franklin Roosevelt in 1938, raised money to fund efforts to find a cure.

Using the method of growing viruses on tissue discovered by John Franklin Enders in 1949, Dr. Jonas Salk developed a vaccine using inactive viruses of the known three strains of polio virus. After Salk's vaccine proved itself safe and effective in field trials in 1954, mass inoculation began immediately. Later, Dr. Albert Sabin developed an oral vaccine against polio, which was released in 1961. Thanks to these highly effective vaccines, polio is no longer a threat to American children, and the World Health Organization is working to eradicate the disease worldwide.

An estimated 250,000 Americans who survived the polio epidemic of the forties and fifties now suffer from what is called "post-polio syndrome." The symptoms of this syndrome include joint pain, a decrease in endurance, and muscle atrophy. The nerves damaged by polio do not regenerate. Doctors believe that because of this, the normal effects of aging occur at a faster rate in polio survivors, causing post-polio syndrome.

Suggested Activities

Polio Patients President Franklin Delano Roosevelt contracted polio in adulthood. Violinist Itzhak Perlman had polio as a child. Choose one of these individuals and report on his life after polio.

Immunizations Write the following words on the chalkboard: measles, rubella, mumps, chicken pox, tetanus, smallpox, diphtheria, whooping cough. In small groups, research the effects of each disease, its prevention, and treatment.

March of Dimes Although the fight against polio has been won, The March of Dimes Foundation continues to work for children's health. Research what the organization is currently doing and develop an action list of ways to help.

References

Crofford, Emily. *Healing Warrior: A Story About Sister Elizabeth Kenny*. Carolrhoda, 1989.
Kehret, Peg. *The Year I Got Polio*. Albert Whitman, 1996.
Weaver, Lydia. *Close to Home: A Story of the Polio Epidemic*. Viking, 1993.

The Mystery of DNA

If you have ever wondered why you have brown skin or curly hair, you have only to look to your biological parents for answers. When you were conceived, cells from the male and female united to form a new organism. Within each of those cells are thin threads called chromosomes which are made up of DNA (deoxyribonucleic acid). Part of these cells are genes. It is the genes which tell your body how to develop. Genes carry coded information about the characteristics of the parents, like the size and shape of the nose, or whether a person is right or left-handed.

Although genes had been identified as early as the 1800s by Austrian monk Gregor Mendel, it was not known what the genes were composed of or how they worked. It was not until 1944 that scientists discovered that the DNA contained in the chromosomes carried the genetic message. During the 1950s a team of scientists, Watson and Crick, was able to build a model of the DNA molecule. Each molecule consists of millions of atoms arranged in a double helix (spiral shape) held together by cross pieces (see diagram). The order in which the atoms are arranged determines the code of genetic information which is then passed on to the next generation. Today, scientists have developed a technique called *genetic fingerprinting,* which can be used to track criminals and study diseases. Also in the experimental stages is genetic engineering which will offer a method for altering the genes and thus changing the characteristics of an organism.

Suggested Activities

Activity On the lines below make a list of at least 30 physical and personality characteristics that are determined by genes. Be specific, e.g. foot size, shape of a mole, etc., rather than general: looks, personality.

_____   _____   _____

_____   _____   _____

_____   _____   _____

_____   _____   _____

_____   _____   _____

_____   _____   _____

_____   _____   _____

_____   _____   _____

_____   _____   _____

_____   _____   _____

Two Female Physicists

During the 1950s two female scientists carried on important work in the field of physics. Rosalyn Yalow and Chien-Shiung Wu were from very different backgrounds, yet both made great contributions to their respective fields. Here is a brief look at these women.

Rosalyn Yalow, Medical Physicist

Rosalyn Yalow

Rosalyn Sussman was born on July 19, 1921, in the Bronx, New York, to poor, European immigrants. After graduating from Hunter College, she went on to study physics. In 1943 she married a colleague, Aaron Yalow, and later had two children. After teaching at Hunter College, Rosalyn Yalow was asked to join a team at the VA Hospital to explore how isotopes could be used in medicine. Along with her long-time lab partner, Solomon R. Berson, Yalow showed how radioactive iodine could be used to treat overactive thyroids and thyroid cancer. Together, they developed the RIA (radioimmunoassay) method, which can detect small amounts of substances in the blood, including vitamins, poison in corpses, and drugs in human hair. RIA is also useful in the diagnosis of diabetes and some types of cancer. In 1977 Rosalyn Yalow won the Noble Prize for Medicine.

Chien-Shiung Wu, Experimental Physicist

Chien-Shiung Wu

In 1936 Chien-Shiung Wu left her native China to study physics in the United States. A brilliant student, Wu attended the University of California at Berkeley where she received her Ph.D. and became an expert on nuclear fission. After marrying in 1942, Wu and her husband, also a physicist, moved to New York City where she worked on the Manhattan Project to build the atomic bomb. Following that project, Wu worked with two doctors, Lee and Yang, who were collaborating on a theory to disprove the law of conservation of parity. Although Lee and Yang won the 1957 Nobel Prize for Physics for their work, Wu was not included. However, she received many other honors of her own, including the first honorary doctorate awarded to a woman by Princeton University and the National Medal of Science.

Suggested Activities

Research Research five more facts about these two scientists. A good resource is *Extraordinary Women Scientists* by Darlene R. Stille (Students Press Inc., 1995).

Discussion Discuss the function of the Manhattan Project and some of the other scientists involved, including the roles of Albert Einstein and Robert Oppenheimer.

Three *Sputniks* and *Explorer I*

For years scientists around the world had envisioned artificial satellites that could circle the earth. Their goals were to collect new information about the earth and our solar system and to transmit messages via satellite. Both the USSR and the United States played a key role in the development of these orbiting spacecrafts. Here is a look at the beginning of the satellite in world history.

On October 4, 1957, the Soviet Union launched *Sputnik I*, the world's first artificial satellite. A small metal ball, the aircraft weighed only 184 pounds and contained a radio transmitter that sent out a steady beep-beep to reveal its location. Barely one month later, on November 3, 1957, the Soviets launched a second satellite, *Sputnik II*, which weighed 1,120 pounds, almost six times as much as the original *Sputnik*. *Sputnik II* carried a dog named Laika, which was the first animal in space. The data that was collected on Laika's behavior during the launch and subsequent days in orbit was used to begin plans for a future manned spaceflight.

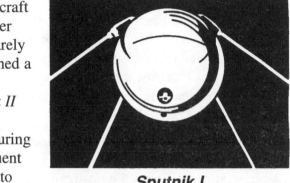
Sputnik I

The third *Sputnik* was sent into orbit on May 15, 1958. The most massive of the three spacecrafts, *Sputnik III* weighed 2,926 pounds. On board was a geophysical laboratory which collected and transmitted information about solar radiation, the earth's magnetic field, and charged particles in the earth's atmosphere.

In January of 1958 between the launchings of *Sputniks II* and *III*, the U.S. launched *Explorer I*. Although it was extremely light, weighing only 11 pounds (4.95 kg), its scientific capabilities were greater than any of the *Sputniks*. *Explorer I* was equipped to measure atmospheric temperature, radiation levels, and cosmic ray intensities. One important result of this test was the discovery of the existence of radiation belts called Van Allen belts that surround the earth. With this launch, the U.S. space program was on its way.

Explorer I

Research Topics

This is not the end of the satellite story. Much of our daily information and communication is derived from satellites. Choose a topic from the list below and write a short report about it.

- The Hubble Space Telescope and its exploration in space
- Antisatellites which are used by the military
- Van Allen belts and their function
- Communications satellites for television, radio, and telephone
- The use of satellites to predict weather conditions
- How satellites are launched and are able to stay up

Mighty Microchip

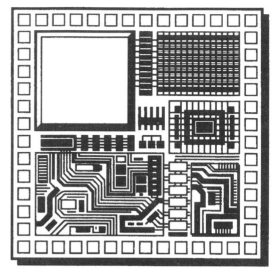

In 1958 engineer Jack Kilby received a patent for the monolithic integrated circuit. Commonly called a microchip, the integrated circuit is the foundation of modern electronics and revolutionized the way we live. The microchip is the heart of a vast array of consumer products from toys to computers. Despite its minuscule size it is a powerful piece of equipment and is capable of carrying out very complex tasks. When the microchip became commercially available in 1961, it was expensive to produce, and, by today's standards, limited in function. Advances in technology have made microchips both common and more complex.

A modern microchip is as thick as a thumbnail, perfectly square, and only one-quarter of an inch (.635 cm) long. Each tiny piece of silicon contains resistors, transistors and capacitors which are connected by a network of miniature circuit lines etched on the surface. A single chip may contain millions of transistors in intricate patterns. To see these patterns clearly, you would need a microscope or strong magnifying glass. The diagram at right will give you some idea of what is on the surface of a computer chip. Note that this is an enlarged drawing.

A microchip can do more work, and at a faster rate, than anything before it could do. Because the microchip uses small amounts of electricity, does not get hot, and costs less to run, it has been possible to reduce the size and cost of computers and other electronic devices.

Microchips can be found in any number of household appliances and everyday things in our lives. Circle the names of all the objects in the box below that contain a microchip.

calculator	cash register	fountain pen
computer	factory robot	microwave
video game	digital watch	radio
emissions control	automatic camera	TV remote control
thermostat	blender	VCR
battery-operated flashlight	heart pacemaker	video camera
camcorder	traffic signals	infrared sensor

Research Topics

Here are some topics for further research.

1. What is silicon and where it can be found?

2. How are conductors, insulators, and semiconductors different?

3. How is a microchip made? How does it work?

New Technology for the Fifties

On this page you will find some interesting information about the scientific and technological advances made during the 1950s. As you research the decade, add to this list.

1950

The first kidney transplant surgery is performed.
Electricity is generated for the first time by nuclear fission, in Idaho Falls, Idaho.
The DC-6 passenger plane is developed.

1951

UNIVAC, the first commercial computer, is manufactured.
An underwater television camera is invented by Jacques Cousteau, French oceanographer.
The field ion microscope is invented; it can picture individual atoms.

1952

The first hydrogen fusion bomb (H-bomb) is tested by the U.S. in the Marshall Islands.
Dr. Virginia Apgar introduces the Apgar Score which measures five crucial aspects in a newborn's health.
The Cinerama widescreen process is developed by Fred Waller.
The first 3-D movies are shown in theaters.

1953

The maser is invented by American physicist Charles H. Townes.
On May 18 Jackie Cochran becomes the first woman to break the sound barrier.
The double helix structure of DNA is discovered by the team of Crick and Watson.

1954

Dr. Jonas Salk develops a vaccine to guard against polio.
The first nuclear submarine, the *Nautilus,* is launched.
RCA markets the first color television.
Robert Moog invents an electronic instrument called a Moog synthesizer.

1955

The first frozen TV dinners are introduced.
The DC 7 passenger plane is developed.
Optical fiber is invented by Dr. Narinder Kapany of England.

1956

The first transatlantic phone cable is installed.
The first nuclear power plant is built.
Dr. Albert Sabin develops an oral polio vaccine.

1957

The Soviet Union launches *Sputnik*, the first artificial satellite.
The Boeing 707 passenger plane is developed.

1958

The first United States' satellite, *Explorer I*, is launched.

Engineer Jack Kilby invents the first integrated circuit, or microchip.

Stereophonic recordings come into use.

Van Allen radiation belts around the earth are discovered.
Arthur Shanlow and Charles Townes patent the laser. The name is an acronym for light amplification by stimulated emission of radiation.

1959

The bathyscaphe *Trieste* descends seven miles into the Mariana Trench.
Anthropologist Mary Leakey discovers skull fragments from early ancestors of modern man in Africa.
The Soviet Union launches *Lunik 2* which makes a hard landing on the moon.

E. B. White

During the 1950s young children enjoyed the stories of such authors as Dr. Seuss, Robert McCloskey (*A Time of Wonder*), and Ludwig Bemelmans (*Madeline* books). Older children read books such as *Amos Fortune, Free Man* by Elizabeth Yates, *Carry On, Mr. Bowditch* by Jean Lee Latham, and *The Witch of Blackbird Pond* by Elizabeth George Speare. In addition to these fine authors, one other writer from the fifties era emerged as a children's favorite for generations to come: E. B. White, author of *Charlotte's Web*. Learn something about White by reading the following paragraphs and filling in the blanks with the correct words from the box below. Share your completed page with a partner.

E. B. White

Elwyn Brooks White, better known as E. B. White, was born on July 11, 1899, in 1._____, New York. The youngest of six children, he had a normal 2._____, yet he often felt lonely. In school he proved to be a good student and won two 3._____ to college. He chose to attend Cornell University where he worked on the *Cornell Daily Sun*, was elected 4._____ of the newspaper in his junior year, and became 5._____ of his fraternity. After graduation, White took a series of editing and 6._____ jobs and eventually went to work part-time for the *New Yorker*. In 1929 his first two books were 7._____ and he married fellow worker Katherine Angell.

Not until 1939 did E. B. White begin writing his first 8._____ book, *Stuart Little*. It would be six more years, however, before it was published. This novel was followed in 1952 by his well-known work, 9._____. White's third children's book, *Trumpet of the Swan*, was written in 1969.

In between children's stories, White kept busy writing books for 10._____ including a 11._____ for writers, *The Elements of Style*. During his lifetime he was personally honored with the Presidential Medal of 12._____. Numerous 13._____ were also given to him for his writing, the most prestigious of which was the 14._____ Honor Award for *Charlotte's Web*. E. B. White who died of Alzheimer's 15._____ on October 1, 1985, has remained a perennial favorite children's author.

president	Freedom	Mount Vernon	children's	editor in chief
awards	guidebook	*Charlotte's Web*	published	scholarships
childhood	Newbery	writing	disease	adults

The Beat Movement

Although life was good for most people during the fifties, not everyone was content. Some people, particularly American writers and artists, participated in what became known as the Beat Movement. Concentrated mostly in Greenwich Village in New York, San Francisco, and Los Angeles, the Beats were rebellious at heart and had a contempt for conformity. Members of the Beat generation questioned the values of their elders, mainly through their words. They would gather at coffee houses and recite original poems about their social disillusionment. Their literature celebrated freedom and spontaneity and was influenced by jazz, drugs, and Asian religions. At the forefront of this movement was Jack Kerouac who provided the voice for the Beat Generation.

Jack Kerouac

Jean Louis Kerouac, later known simply as Jack Kerouac, was born on March 12, 1922, in Lowell, Massachusetts. After high school he studied briefly at Columbia University and served for a while in the merchant marines. Following those experiences he worked at odd jobs and traveled extensively throughout the United States. It was his travels and his accounts of his adventures that would bring him fame.

Kerouac wrote of his journeys in a highly personal style, one that employed spontaneous and unconventional prose. In his best-known novel, *On the Road*, he described his life of freedom from conventional middle-class ties and values. Through his characters Kerouac explored the enjoyment of nature and the senses and the freedom from responsibility. Although they have no particular place to go, the characters travel for the adventure and the pleasure of change.

Kerouac's writing contributed to his position as the leading spokesperson of the Beat Generation, and he became the epitome of the Beat lifestyle. Following his success with *On the Road*, Kerouac wrote a series of similarly structured novels. His last book, *Big Sur*, was written in 1962. Jack Kerouac died on October 21, 1969, in St. Petersburg, Florida.

Suggested Activities

Others Allen Ginsberg and Lawrence Ferlinghetti were two other Beat writers of the fifties. Find out five facts about each of these authors.

Forerunners The Beat movement also advocated peace and civil rights. Discuss how the movement's values set the stage for the radical protests of the 1960s.

Compare Compare and contrast the writers of the Beat movement with mainstream fifties writers such as J. D. Salinger, James Baldwin, and James Michener.

Jasper Johns

Abstract Expressionism was an art form that debuted in the late 1940s and continued into the early fifties. Pioneered by such artists as Hans Hoffman and Jackson Pollock, Abstract Expressionist works were noted for their lack of recognizable images. During the 1950s Jasper Johns began to break away from this type of art and forged the way into Pop Art. In his pieces he would take a familiar two-dimensional object as a subject and present it in an uncommon way. Johns' *Three Flags*, for example, stacks three U.S. flags in decreasing sizes. Although the flag is realistically portrayed, the overall picture provides the viewer with a new and different way of looking at the flag.

Jasper Johns was born in the South in the year 1930. He studied art at the University of South Carolina and in the early 1950s worked as a commercial artist in New York City. One of his earliest successes was a window display for the well-known jewelry store, Tiffany's. In the window he arranged actual diamonds among real potatoes and dirt.

Today, Jasper Johns is acknowledged as one of the most famous and esteemed living artists. In addition to painting, Johns also does printmaking and some sculpting. His hallmark is presenting common objects, from flags to numbers to maps, in unusual ways.

Art Project

Create an art project, using Jasper Johns's style by following the directions below.

Materials:

drawing paper or typing paper; rubber stamps of numerals 0–9 and ink pad; colored pencils or crayons

Directions:

Fold a sheet of paper into sixteenths and crease it along the folds. Unfold the paper. Use the stamps to make a different numeral from 0 to 9 in each space. Shade the numerals with black or complementary colors to add depth.

Frank Lloyd Wright

Although Frank Lloyd Wright was born in the nineteenth century, his ideas and architecture were far ahead of their time. His innovative contributions to the American home included these features: cathedral ceilings, built-in furniture and lighting fixtures, carports, and massive fireplaces. In architectural design he offered layouts which flowed seamlessly from room to room and seemed to merge with the outside environment. Perhaps his best example in this area is the Kaufmann House in Bear Run, Pennsylvania. Its lines flow out of the surrounding rock while cantilevered terraces angle out over a running waterfall. Even now Wright's buildings fit right in with current modern lines. One of his most famous designs, the Guggenheim Museum, was considered radical when it was completed in 1959, yet the structure's curves give it a modern, abstract, and almost timeless look.

Frank Lloyd Wright

Not only was Wright's architecture radical, his whole life seemed to be dedicated to outraging the public. From his well-publicized bankruptcies to his scandalous divorces and relationships, he remained newsworthy throughout his 70-year career. A self-assured man, Wright's goal was to be the greatest architect who had yet lived. Indeed, his unique designs are testament to his great genius.

Suggested Activities

Building Blocks Consider this bit of information: All Frank Lloyd Wright remembers about elementary school was building with blocks. How might building with blocks have helped shape Wright's future architectural career? In small groups, build block structures in the style of Frank Lloyd Wright.

Innovations Discuss the contributions Frank Lloyd Wright made to the American home. For homework, find examples of each contribution in your homes or neighborhood or find pictures in old magazines.

Guest Speaker Invite a local architect to your class to speak about the facets of an architect's life, what high school classes are helpful and necessary, the tools used, and so forth. In small groups, prepare possible interview questions ahead of time.

The Roots of Rock and Roll

Students may think that rock and roll was always around, but there was a time when it was not here to stay. Below is a brief history of rock and roll in the U.S.A.

By the mid fifties, popular music in the United States was in a rut with bland tunes and monotonous rhythms. Music charts were dominated by white musicians, but increasingly artists were recording softer versions of popular black songs. A breakthrough occurred when "Rock Around the Clock," a single by Bill Haley and the Comets, was used in the film *The Blackboard Jungle*. Haley recognized a growing trend among white teenagers to listen to black music stations. While Haley's idea was correct, his image was not enough to earn him teen-idol status. That honor was left to up-and-coming artist Elvis Presley. With his shy smile and swiveling hips, Elvis captured the hearts and souls of American teens. His music opened doors for other artists, both black and white, to show their talents. Memorable among them are Jerry Lee Lewis, Fats Domino, Little Richard, Chuck Berry, and Buddy Holly.

Fats Domino Fats Domino, a heavy-set musician, played piano and sang. "Blueberry Hill" is probably his most-remembered hit.

Jerry Lee Lewis

Little Richard Little Richard, well-known for "Tutti Frutti" and "Good Golly Miss Molly," was the most outrageous of the pianists. He was noted for his frenetic playing, wild screams, and energetic performances.

Jerry Lee Lewis Jerry Lee Lewis followed in Fats Domino's and Little Richard's footsteps with his piano-pounding ways and electrifying vocals. Both "Whole Lotta Shakin' Goin' On" and "Great Balls of Fire" remain rock and roll classics.

Chuck Berry Chuck Berry, the only non-piano player of the four, was almost twenty-six before he gave his first paid performance. His first hit, "Maybelline," came in 1956 and was followed by rock and roll classics like "Johnny B. Goode" and "Roll Over Beethoven." Berry is noted for his famous shuffle while playing the guitar. Today, Berry still performs and has had one of the longest careers in rock and roll.

Chuck Berry

Buddy Holly Buddy Holly's hits included "That'll Be the Day" and "Peggy Sue." His meteoric rise in the music industry came to an abrupt end in a plane crash on February 3, 1959, near Mason City, Iowa. Also killed in the crash were Ritchie Valens, an up-and-coming singer whose two best-selling songs were "Donna" and "La Bamba," and J. P. Richardson, known as "The Big Bopper," of "Chantilly Lace" fame.

The Roots of Rock and Roll *(cont.)*

Elvis Presley Elvis Presley has been called an idol, an icon, and a legend, but he was indisputably the King of rock and roll. Born on January 8, 1935, in Tupelo, Mississippi, Presley won his first talent contest when he was just eight years old. In 1954 he recorded his first song as a present for his mother. The owner of the recording service had recently started his own record company, Sun, and signed Presley as a new talent. Presley did not have much commercial success with Sun and after a year left for RCA. Thanks in large part to television exposure and appearances on programs such as *The Ed Sullivan Show*, Presley became a huge star all across America. His hip movements and gyrations, however, were cropped from the viewers' sight.

In 1955 Colonel Tom Parker became Presley's manager and signed him to RCA Records at a cost of $40,000. One year later Presley had a number one hit with "Heartbreak Hotel." The same week that it reached number one in the U.S., it also achieved its millionth sale. Eventually, the song also became number one in Great Britain. A string of hits continued with "Hound Dog," "Don't Be Cruel," and "Love Me Tender."

Presley entered the film industry and starred in a number of musicals until he was drafted by the U.S. Army. For two years he served his country, and he was proud to do so. His return to civilian life meant a return to acting, but his singing career was not as hot as it once was. Pop artists of the sixties began to replace his now dated style.

During the seventies, Presley started live tours, and his singing career picked up. Yet his self-destructive lifestyle was catching up with him. On August 16, 1977, Elvis Presley died in Memphis of heart failure caused by prescription drug abuse. He left behind an impressive 94 gold singles and over 40 gold albums. Today, he remains one of the biggest influences on 20th century pop culture and is an enduring idol in the world of rock and roll.

Suggested Activity

Rating the Songs Listen to one of the songs spotlighted above or another song from the fifties. On the chart below, rate the song.

Song Title: _____

Artist: _____

Score (circle one)

    60   65   70   75   80   85   90   95   100

Reasons (check all that apply):

    I like the words.   I like the beat.

    I like the artist.   It's easy to dance to.

Other _____

_____

New to the Fifties

Among the new inventions of the fifties were 3-D movies, the Hula-Hoop, Frisbees, drive-in movie theaters, and the microchip. In addition are two more familiar brand names: Jif Peanut Butter and WD-40. Below you will find a brief history of these two common household items.

Jif Peanut Butter

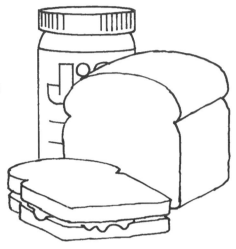

History Peanuts crushed into a paste has been around for centuries—Incas and African tribes ate such a food. In 1890 a doctor made a peanut paste for his geriatric patients with bad teeth. Several brands of peanut butter were on the market by 1914, but after Jif was introduced in 1956, it became the best-selling peanut butter in America. The name Jif is short for "jiffy," the time it takes to make a peanut butter sandwich.

Interesting Facts Jif comes in a number of varieties, including creamy, crunchy, and reduced fat. An opened jar of Jif peanut butter will remain fresh for three months. There are 1,218 peanuts in the typical 28-ounce jar of Jif.

Activity Taste test a number of brands of peanut butter. Have them vote on their favorites. In groups, make a graph of the results.

WD-40

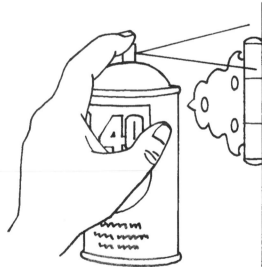

History During the early 1950s, the aerospace industry began looking for a product to eliminate moisture from electrical circuitry and to prevent corrosion on airplanes. A satisfactory product was invented by Norman Larsen who was the president and head chemist at the Rocket Chemical Company. His water displacement formula was developed on his fortieth try, thus the name WD-40. When it was discovered that WD-40 worked well to quiet squeaky doors and unstick stuck locks, a number of employees began sneaking the product home. In 1958 the product was made available to the public.

Interesting Facts The WD-40 Company makes more than one million gallons of the lubricant each year. When astronaut John Glenn circled the earth in *Friendship VII* in 1964, the spacecraft was covered with WD-40 from top to bottom.

Activity WD-40 can be found in four out of five American homes. Test the validity of this statistic. For homework, check to see if WD-40 is available in your home. Tally the number of homes in which the product was present. Compare that figure with the total number of students who participated in the poll. Does the statistic hold up?

Toys of the Fifties

Many of the toys that were invented in the fifties are still around today and in a big way. Take a look at three toys with which you are probably familiar.

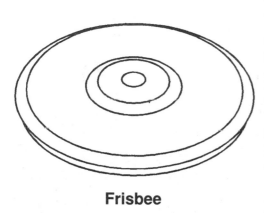

Frisbee

Frisbee The Frisbee story began in the late 1800s with the Frisbie Pie Company in Bridgeport, Connecticut. Their pies, which came in a ten-inch-wide round tin with a raised edge and wide brim, were popular with students at nearby Yale University. At some point, pie-tin catch had become a fad among the young collegians. The fad continued into the 1950s but was changed forever with the introduction of a plastic flying disk called Flyin' Saucer, invented by Walter Frederick Morrison. First marketed as the Pluto Platter, the toy's name was officially changed to Frisbee when Wham-O's president saw Yale students throwing and catching Frisbie pie plates. However, not until the 1960s did sales of the Frisbee take off. Today it remains a popular toy and sport.

Activity Conduct an aluminum pie plate throwing contest. Contrast the flying characteristics of pie plates with the plastic Frisbee.

Hula-Hoop Besides the Frisbee, the Wham-O toy company also manufactured the Hula-Hoop. For six months it enjoyed great success as the Hula-Hoop became the fastest-selling toy in history. Just as quickly, however, the craze seemed to die down. Every generation since then has seen a resurgence of the unusual toy. Based on a wooden hoop used by Australian youths, the plastic Hula-Hoop was invented by Richard Knerr, a partner in the Wham-O toy manufacturing company.

Activity Invent a new game to play with the Hula-Hoop. Teach a friend how to play the game.

Hula-Hoop

Barbie Doll In 1959 the Barbie Doll made her debut. Today, she is the best-selling toy in American history. Her inventor is Ruth Handler, a former secretary and housewife. Ruth noticed that her daughter preferred to play with teenage dolls rather than those designed for her own age group. The problem was that the teenage dolls available at that time were paper cutouts. Ruth designed a more grown-up doll that would wear fashionable clothing and be a little girl's dream of things to come. Barbie, named after Handler's daughter, made her debut at the 1959 New York Toy Show. A huge success, it sold $500 million worth in its first eight years. Ruth Handler went on to become vice-president and then president of Mattel, Inc., the company that manufactures Barbie.

Activity Design a new outfit for a Barbie from a past era.

Dressing for the Fifties

Young people during the fifties were expected to dress much like their elders and according to their gender. Girls, for example, could wear full skirts with petticoats or pencil-slim skirts and sweater sets. Boys typically wore a shirt, tie, and pressed trousers. See more fashions for teens of the fifties on this and the next page.

Typical Clothing for Girls

a man's shirt worn outside
of dungarees (jeans)
penny loafers

Peter Pan collared blouse
full skirts and petticoats
(poodle skirts)

pencil-slim skirt

Dressing for the Fifties *(cont.)*

Typical Clothing for Boys

Hawaiian shirts with
Bermuda shorts

shirt, tie, and pressed
trousers
penny loafers
crewcut

jeans, leather jacket
hair slicked back into a
ducktail

Elsewhere...

This chronology gives a few of the important events around the globe during the 1950s. Have students research further any people and events that interest them.

1950
- British inventor Chris Cockerell invents the hovercraft.
- China and the Soviet Union sign the Sino-Soviet Pact naming the U.S. and Japan as mutual enemies.
- North Korea invades South Korea.
- Russia announces it has an atom bomb.

1951
- The first underwater TV camera is developed by Frenchman Jacques Cousteau.
- The Suez Canal crisis takes place.
- Chinese forces occupy Tibet.
- Juan Perón is re-elected president of Argentina.
- Libya becomes an independent state.
- The first Miss World Contest is staged.

1952
- The Bonn Convention is held; Britain, France, and the U.S. end occupation of West Germany.
- The Mau Mau uprising begins in Kenya, Africa.
- Egypt ousts King Farouk.
- King George VI dies and is succeeded by Queen Elizabeth II.
- Eva Perón dies of cancer in Argentina.
- The first national elections are held in India.

1953
- Sir Edmund Hillary and Tenzing Norgay are the first climbers to reach the top of Mt. Everest.
- Stalin dies.
- Tito becomes president of Yugoslavia.
- Ian Fleming publishes the first of his twelve James Bond novels.
- Crick and Watson develop the first model of the structure of DNA.
- The Queen of England is crowned.

1954
- Roger Bannister of England runs a mile in under four minutes; the first man to do so.
- SEATO (Southeast Asia Treaty Organization) is formed.

1955
- Churchill resigns as prime minister of England.
- South Vietnam becomes a republic.
- Argentine dictator Juan Perón is overthrown.

1956
- The Warsaw Pact is signed by the Soviet Union and the countries it dominates.
- Nasser is elected president of Egypt.
- Khrushchev, the new Soviet prime minister, denounces Stalin.
- Transatlantic cable telephone service is inaugurated.
- The Suez Crisis ends when Britain and France withdraw troops from Egypt.
- Students in Hungary rebel against the Soviet government.

1957
- Laika, a female Samoyed, becomes the first animal in space.
- *Sputnik I* is launched by the USSR, followed by *Sputnik II*.
- The Gold Coast of Africa becomes Ghana.
- Malaya becomes independent.
- The Soviet Union launches an Intercontinental Ballistic Missile (ICBM).

1958
- Charles de Gaulle returns to power as the first president of France's Fifth Republic.
- Egypt and Syria form the United Arab Republic.
- John XXIII becomes the new Pope.
- China crushes the national uprising in Tibet.

1959
- Castro overthrows Batista's government and gains control of Cuba.
- Singapore becomes independent.
- Anthropologist Mary Leakey discovers skull fragments from early ancestors of modern humans in east Africa.
- Mao unites his country.
- The bathyscaphe *Trieste* descends seven miles down to the Mariana Trench in the Pacific Ocean.
- The Soviet Union launches *Lunik 2* which makes a hard landing on the moon.
- The Antarctic Treaty is signed by twelve nations.
- The Dalai Lama flees from Tibet.

Olympics of the Fifties

During the fifties the world was at peace, and the Olympics were back on track. Two Olympiads were held—in 1952 and 1956. Read some interesting facts about each of these competitions.

1952

Summer Games at Helsinki, Finland

- The winner of the Olympic decathlon is considered the world's best athlete. In 1952 that honor went to Bob Mathias who, at age 17, became the youngest man to earn the gold medal in the event.
- A 29-year old Czechoslovakian military officer, Emil Zatopek, mesmerized the crowd at Helsinki. After winning the 5,000-meter run he watched as his wife, Dana, won the women's javelin. Then he announced that he would enter the marathon despite the fact that he had never before run a marathon. Zapotek easily upstaged his United States and Soviet rivals. In winning the race he became the first runner since Hannes Kolehmainen of Finland in 1912 to win both the 5,000 and 10,000 in one Olympics.
- At the age of 32, Korean American Sammy Lee became the oldest athlete ever to win an Olympic diving medal.

Winter Games at Oslo, Norway

- A record thirty nations competed in the Norway Olympics.
- American figure skater Dick Button performed the first-ever triple rotation jump; he won the men's singles figure skating event.
- A controversy arose over the size of the German bobsled teams who won the two-man and four-man races. The International Bobsleigh Federation changed its rules and limited the weight of teams to allow for fair competition in subsequent Olympics.

1956

Summer Games at Melbourne, Australia

- The summer games were held in late November since that is summer in the Southern Hemisphere.
- Bobby Morrow, a United States sprinter, won gold in the 100-and 200-meter races and added a third as a member of the 4 x 100 relay.
- A surprising moment occurred while the Soviets and Hungary were playing water polo. The game was stopped when a Hungarian player was cut in the eye by a hit from a Soviet player. During the time-out the Russians decided to forfeit the game.
- During the closing ceremonies of these games, the athletes intermingled instead of marching by national teams.

Winter Games at Cortina, Italy

- In 1956 Tony Sailer became the hero of Austria as the first skier to sweep gold medals in all three alpine events: the downhill, slalom, and giant slalom.
- Hayes Alan Jenkins and Tenley Albright of the United States won gold medals in men's and womens' figure skating, respectively.

Suggested Activities

Events In small groups, make a list of all the sports and events conducted at either the summer Olympics or winter Olympics. Describe each event.

Research Fnd out and list all Olympic sporting events that feature mixed competition.

Passages

Births

1950
- Olympic swimmer Mark Spitz
- actresses Cybill Sheperd and Holly Hunter
- talk-show host Jay Leno

1951
- actors Kurt Russell, Michael Keaton, Tony Danza, and Mark Harmon
- singers Stevie Wonder and Luther Vandross
- first American woman to orbit the earth, Sally Ride

1952
- actors Robin Williams, Dan Aykroyd, Jeff Goldblum, and David Hasselhoff
- singer Tom Petty

1953
- Amy Tan, author of best-selling novels
- singer Michael Bolton
- actors Alfre Woodard and Pierce Brosnan
- supermodel Christie Brinkley

1954
- radio host Howard Stern
- tennis player Chris Evert
- actors John Travolta and Denzel Washington
- comic Jerry Seinfeld

1955
- Yo Yo Ma, world-famous cellist
- actors Arsenio Hall and Bruce Willis
- singer Billy Idol
- Apple Computer founder Steven Jobs
- lawyer and novelist John Grisham

1956
- Dorothy Hamill, Olympic gold medal winning figure skater
- actor Mel Gibson
- football great Joe Montana
- tennis great Bjorn Borg
- boxing champion Sugar Ray Leonard
- software magnate William H. Gates III

1957
- singers Gloria Estefan and Holly Dunn
- television journalist Katie Couric
- game-show celebrity Vanna White

1958
- actors Annette Bening, Sharon Stone, Alec Baldwin, Keenan Ivory Wayans, and Jimmy Smits

1959
- singers Sade, Madonna, and Randy Travis
- tennis great John McEnroe
- basketball great Magic Earvin Johnson

Deaths

1950
- Charles Richard Drew, scientist who showed how to preserve blood
- Edna St. Vincent Millay, poet
- British author George Orwell

1951
- author Sinclair Lewis
- newspaper magnate William Randolph Hearst

1952
- Shipwreck Kelly, professional stuntman who started flagpole sitting fad
- philosopher John Dewey
- Eva Perón, wife of Argentine leader Juan Perón
- Margaret Wise Brown, children's author

1953
- Jim Thorpe, a great athlete and Olympic winner
- Hank Williams, country western singer
- playwright Eugene O'Neill and writer Dylan Thomas

1954
- French artist Henri Matisse
- Enrico Fermi, Italian-born physicist
- Artist Frida Kahlo

1955
- Albert Einstein, one of the world's greatest geniuses
- James Dean, actor and teen idol
- African American civil rights activist Mary McLeod Bethune
- Matthew Henson, North Pole explorer
- Alexander Fleming, the discoverer of penicillin

1956
- Mildred Babe Didrikson Zaharias, Olympic athlete and sportswoman
- A.A. Milne, children's author

1957
- actor Humphrey Bogart
- Admiral Richard E. Byrd, polar explorer
- artist Diego Rivera
- Gabriela Mistral, Latin America's only winner of a Nobel Prize in literature

1958
- actor Tyrone Power

1959
- rock 'n' roll pioneer Buddy Holly and singers Ritchie Valens and J.P. Richardson, the "Big Bopper"
- opera singer Mario Lanza
- blues singer Billie Holliday

The St. Lawrence Seaway

In 1954 Canada and the United States began a joint project to build a waterway linking the Atlantic Ocean with the Great Lakes. Each country was responsible for building and operating its own sections, but the seaway is important to the economies of both countries. The resulting St. Lawrence Seaway is formed by the St. Lawrence River, several lakes, and a system of canals and locks. Completed in 1959, the seaway extends from the eastern end of Lake Erie to Montreal, Toronto, and Hamilton, in Canada and Buffalo, Cleveland, Detroit, Chicago, and Duluth in the United States.

To learn more facts and figures about this project complete the problems at the beginning of each statement and fill in the blanks with the corresponding answers.

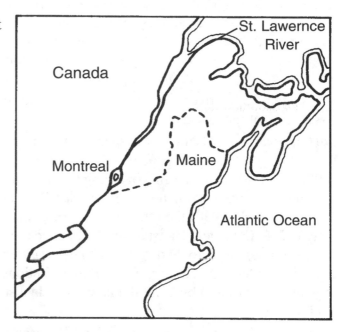

1. 6175 ÷ 95   The canal system of the St. Lawrence Seaway is _____ miles or 105 kilometers long.

2. 2257 ÷ 37   The canals of the St. Lawrence Seaway are all at least 200 feet or _____ meters wide.

3. 1323 ÷ 49   All canals are at least _____ feet or 8 meters deep.

4. 1392 ÷ 58   Locks measure 80 feet or _____ meters wide.

5. 11,417 ÷ 49   Each lock is 766 feet or _____ meters long.

6. 2610 ÷ 87   The locks are _____ feet or 9 meters deep.

7. 1610 ÷ 46   A ship can pass through a lock in approximately _____ minutes.

8. 132 ÷ 88   In good weather, the entire route can be traveled in about _____ days.

9. 2880 ÷ 64   Each year the St. Lawrence Seaway handles about 50 million short tons or _____ million metric tons of cargo.

10. 42,716 ÷ 59   Altogether, the seaway extends about 450 miles or _____ kilometers from the end of Lake Erie to Montreal.

Revolution in Cuba

On January 1, 1959, Fidel Castro seized power from president Fulgencio Batista. Initially the United States supported the new Cuban government but was soon forced to reconsider its political position.

This page gives an overview of events in Cuba during Castro's revolutionary days.

Background As a result of the Spanish-American War, Cuba gained its independence from Spain in 1898. Until it became a self-governing republic in May, 1902, it was governed by the American military. During the early 1930s the effective ruler of Cuba was army officer Fulgencio Batista. In 1952 he took over the government directly and two years later was elected president. A number of anti-Batista factions began to emerge, and by 1958 the island was in a state of civil war.

Fidel Castro

Castro Fidel Castro was a lawyer who led a group of well-armed revolutionaries in widespread warfare against the government. The attacks began in 1956 and were based in the mountains of Oriente Province. On January 1, 1959, Castro and his troops marched into the capital of Havana and seized control from the corrupt Batista. Few Cubans opposed the coup.

Conditions Under Batista's cruel dictatorship the rich had become richer, but the poor had not fared as well. Although luxury houses, gambling casinos, and Cadillacs were plentiful in Havana, most Cubans were starving and penniless. Jobs were scarce and there were no unemployment benefits or health care.

Initial Response Initially, the United States was supportive of the young Castro, and he was given a fine welcome on his arrival in Washington, D.C., in April 1959. The U.S. was pleased to learn that he would hold free elections in Cuba. Castro was sworn in as prime minister in February. Manuel Urrutía was the president.

Rethinking In July of 1959 Castro dismissed Urrutía and made himself president of Cuba. He began to divide and distribute large sugar plantations among Cuban farmers. This worried the U.S. because many of these farms belonged to Americans. For years, the U.S. government had controlled Cuba's economy and imported two-thirds of Cuba's sugar at fixed prices. An even bigger worry was that Fidel Castro seemed to bc lcaning toward communism.

Sixties In 1960 the Cubans accepted $100 million dollars in credit from the Soviet Union. The U.S. bought fewer sugar imports from Cuba. In 1961, a U.S.-backed revolt against Castro's government failed.

Suggested Activities

Research Che Guevara was an Argentinian who devoted his life to fighting corrupt regimes. Research Che's life to learn how he helped Fidel Castro gain control of Cuba.

Continuation What do you know about current U.S.-Cuba relations? Discuss any changes since Fidel first came to power there. Scan the newspapers or the Internet for any new developments.

The Black Pearl

Pelé, born Edson Arantes do Nascimento, was only 17 when he played in his first World Cup of soccer in 1958. Some 60,000 people had jammed into the 50,000-seat arena in Stockholm, in hopes that they would see Sweden win its first world title. The Swedish coach thought his team could win if they scored first. Brazil had a tendency to become disorganized when they trailed in a game. What happened at that game, however, stunned everyone—the spectators, coaches, and players. Pelé inspired his teammates with his enthusiastic and energetic pace. It was his magnificent moves on the field, though, that really wowed the crowd. He displayed such control of his body and such athleticism that even the Swedish fans began to chant his name. After their win, the Brazilian team returned home as national heroes and Pelé was nicknamed "The Black Pearl."

Pelé

Pelé was born on October 23, 1940, in a small town in Minas Gerais state. His father, a soccer player, was pleased with his firstborn and predicted that the boy would grow up to become a great soccer player. As a young child Pelé ran and played with the other students in his neighborhood. They had to use grapefruits or socks filled with rags because there was not enough money for a real soccer ball. Bored with school, he quit in the fourth grade and became a cobbler's apprentice. His free time was spent playing soccer. When he was twelve, he was chosen to play on a junior league where he learned the strategies and tactics of professional soccer. By the time he was 14, he was invited to join a professional team. It meant leaving home and moving to Santos near Brazil's largest city, Sao Paulo. Often he would be homesick, but he kept busy attending school between games and practicing with the team. Soon, people began coming out to the games just to watch this remarkable new player. Then, at age 17 he found himself on the Brazilian World Cup team.

Before the team left for Stockholm, Pelé injured his knee. He was fearful that it would not heal correctly and he would be unable to continue his professional career. Though in pain, he put on an unforgettable performance at the World Cup and led his team to victory. He went on to play until he retired from the Santos team in 1974. For three years after that he played for a team in the newly formed North American Soccer League.

Pelé remains a public figure in his native Brazil. He starred in some movies and recorded a hit song. His future plans may include something in the political arena. Whatever his goals, he remains the most popular soccer player in the history of the game.

Suggested Activities

Records Pelé finished his career with 1,216 goals. Is it still an all-time world record?

Defense Defend this statement: Soccer is the most popular sport in the world.

Independence in Africa

The 1950s were witness to numerous political changes in Africa as more and more countries gained their independence. Read the dates and countries listed in the chart below and label the map with the names of these countries.

Independence Dates	
Year	**Countries**
1951	Libya
1956	Sudan, Morocco, Tunisia
1957	Ghana
1958	Guinea

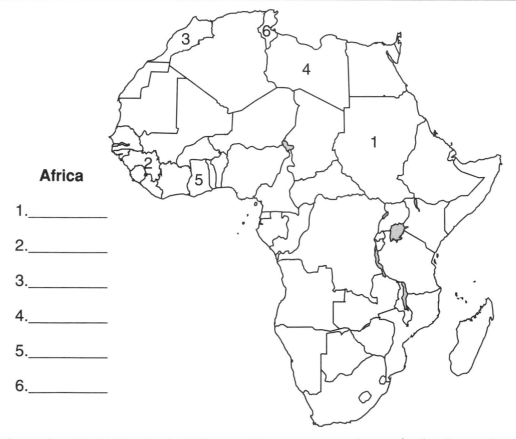

Africa

1._____

2._____

3._____

4._____

5._____

6._____

Activity After World War II, the Kikuyu of Kenya became increasingly dissatisfied with the British rule. In 1952 many of the Kikuyu banded together to form the Mau Mau. Their goal was to drive the Europeans out of their country. Finish this story. Find out how and when the war ended, how long it lasted, and the results.

- -

Answers: (fold under before copying)

1. Sudan 2. Guinea 3. Morocco 4. Libya 5. Ghana 6. Tunisia

The Leakeys

Mary Douglas Nicol became interested in archaeology through her father, Erskine Nicol. Every autumn the family would travel from England to the continent of Europe. At the age of 11, Mary Nicol became fascinated by the Cro-Magnon cave paintings in France. She went on to study archaelology at the university and participated in several digs. Her special area of interest was stone tools. In 1935 Nicol met Louis Leakey. The son of missionaries, Leakey had studied in England and then returned to Africa, where he was raised. The two became friends, and the following Christmas Eve Louis and Mary were married in London. Shortly afterward the couple left for Africa and settled at Olduvai Gorge in Tanzania, a site Leakey had identified.

Louis and Mary Leakey

The two complemented one another in their work. Louis Leakey was most happy lecturing, traveling, and talking with reporters while Mary Leakey enjoyed the actual excavations. To support their digs, Louis Leakey wrote books, gave lectures, and worked as the head of a museum in Nairobi. The couple had three sons who accompanied them on their archaeological excavations whenever possible.

In 1948 Mary Leakey made an important discovery: the skull of a Proconsul, an early ancestor of the chimpanzee, gorilla, and modern human. Her exacting method of digging had paid off, and today all archaeologists in Africa dig shallow layers rather than deep holes. Altogether, the Leakeys and their assistants found more than 2,000 stone tools and numerous mammal bones. Then in July 1959, Mary Leakey spotted some teeth sticking up from the rubble. In the next nineteen days, 400 pieces were carefully excavated from the spot. It took another eighteen months to fit all the pieces together. She had uncovered the Zinjanthropus man, nicknamed the Nutcracker Man. A hominid man-ape fossil, it is believed to be 1,750,000 years old.

This discovery of the earliest man brought the Leakeys much publicity and money for research. They were regularly featured in National Geographic magazine and received many awards. Louis Leakey died in 1972, but Mary Leakey continued her search for fossils until she was well into her eighties.

Suggested Activity

Choose one of the following topics for further research.

- Louis Leakey's sponsorship of Jane Goodall's research on chimpanzees
- Potassium-argon dating, a method of dating artifacts developed in the 50s
- The hoax of the Piltdown man
- Albert Schweitzer's missionary work in Africa
- The importance of the findings at Olduvai Gorge

References

Beakman's Book of Dead Guys and Gals of Science by Luann Colombo (Andrews and McMeel, 1994).

Mary Leakey: In Search of Human Beginnings by Deborah Heiligman (W.H.Freeman and Company, 1995).

Thematic Unit: Archaeology (Teacher Created Materials, #296).

Crisis in the Suez

A crisis occurred at the Suez Canal in 1956 that could have been disastrous if it had not been resolved correctly. On this page are some highlights of the Suez Crisis.

Background After World War II Egypt was in a politically unstable condition. Although it was theoretically an independent nation, it had been dominated by Great Britain for decades. Britain's interest in the country was to protect the Suez Canal and to ensure safe passage to India and the Far East for trade purposes.

Nasser Seizes Control In July of 1952 a group of military officers staged a coup and overthrew Egypt's monarchy, and in 1953 the country became a republic. Colonel Gamal Abdel Nasser, an Arab nationalist, became president of Egypt in 1954. He championed the Arabs' struggle against Israel and drew Egypt into alliance with the Soviet Union and away from the West.

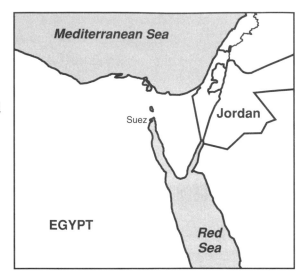

Nationalizing the Canal Historically, the Suez Canal was owned by a corporation dominated by Great Britain and France. In 1954 Britain agreed to gradually withdraw its defense forces, and by June of 1956 British forces were no longer present. On July 26, 1956, Nasser nationalized the canal with the intention of using canal tolls to pay for the construction of the Aswan High Dam on the Nile River.

Secret Plans Great Britain and France feared that Nasser might close the canal to international traffic. They began secret plans to take control of the canal and oust Nasser, if possible. Israel, who allied itself with the plan, sent brigades into Egypt on October 29, 1956, and defeated the Egyptian forces there. A peacekeeping force was sent by Great Britain and France. Egypt sank 40 ships in the canal, blocking it from use.

Response The plan did not work, however, due to public opposition within Great Britain and France. When the Soviets made threats, the intervention stopped. Through the UN a truce was reached in November, and the British, French, and Israelis withdrew on December 22, 1956, ending the Suez Crisis. A UN salvage team cleared the canal, which reopened in 1957.

Results Nasser became a hero to his people. Great Britain's prime minister, Anthony Eden, resigned.

Suggested Activities

Your Opinion What was the United States' stand on the Suez Crisis? How might the crisis have ended if the United States had offered support to Great Britain and France? Write a defense of your argument.

Cartography Find a map which includes Great Britain, France, India, and Egypt. Locate the Suez Canal. Trace and measure a route from Great Britain to India through the Suez Canal; trace and measure a route that ships would have to take if the canal were not open to them. Compare the distances.

Presidential Decisions President Eisenhower refused to support the British and French action against Nasser. If you had been president, what actions would you have taken? Explain your reasons.

Speech Writing After the Suez crisis Britain's prime minister, Anthony Eden, resigned. Write a speech he might have given to the British people, explaining his reasons for resignation.

Claims to Antarctica

During the second decade of the twentieth century, two teams of scientists reached the South Pole. A Norwegian group led by Roald Amundsen arrived there in December 1911 and returned safely. The British team headed by Robert Scott reached the pole in January 1912, but he and his companions died of the cold before they could return. After these explorations some nations sent scientists, biologists, and geologists to study the Antarctic region. A few maintained year-round research stations. By the mid-1950s seven countries had claimed parts of Antarctica as their own territory. The United States had strong interest in the continent but filed no formal claims. All disputes were suspended during an 18-month period in 1957–1958. That time was proclaimed the International Geophysical Year as twelve nations launched a major effort to learn more about the continent. Its success led to the 1959 drafting of the Antarctic Treaty which declared the continent a research preserve. Nations would be free to exchange scientific findings. Furthermore, the area was to be used solely for peaceful purposes. Testing of weapons and disposal of radioactive material on the continent were banned.

Today, large-scale exploration and development is limited by an agreement among 33 nations. Future plans call for the establishment of an Antarctic World Park. Environmentalists worldwide agree that this would provide much-needed protection for the earth's last great wilderness.

A number of specialists are studying different aspects of Antarctic life. Draw lines to match the scientist in Column A with the subject of their studies in Column B.

Column A	**Column B**
1. ornithologists	A. continental ice shelf; glaciers; past climates
2. biologists	B. ecology of Antarctic lakes; glacial meltwater
3. oceanographers	C. how Antarctica affects humans who live there for long periods
4. glaciologists	D. fulmars; Adelie and emperors; rookeries
5. terrestrial biologists	E. weather patterns; radiation; atmosphere
6. medical scientists	F. crude oils; chemical structures
7. meteorologists	G. ice edge; currents; sediments
8. organic geochemists	H. mating rituals; feeding; relationships between animals

Conquering Mount Everest

The sport of mountaineering began in the late 1700s when Frenchman Michel Paccard climbed Mount Blanc in the Alps. For the next 200 years, climbers continued to explore peaks in the Alps as well as mountains in Africa, the Andes in South America, and the Rockies in North America. Only one mountain seemed out of reach: Mount Everest. Located in the Himalayas between Tibet and Nepal, it is the highest mountain in the world at 29,028 feet (8,848 meters).

One main obstacle had to be overcome before a climb could even be attempted. Permission had to be obtained from Tibet or Nepal to travel through their lands. In 1920 a British team was granted permission to enter Tibet. This fact-finding expedition encountered bad weather and strong winds, and all the climbers were affected by altitude sickness. After returning to England, plans were begun for the next expedition. Through the years other attempts to reach the top of Mount Everest were likewise unsuccessful.

Mount Everest

In 1952 Colonel John Hunt was chosen to lead a 1953 expedition to Mount Everest. He mapped the route, made sure there would be enough supplies, purchased the best equipment, and picked the right team members. Among this group was New Zealander Edmund Hillary and a Sherpa northern Nepalese mountaineer named Norgay Tenzing. Following three weeks of training, they began their long, arduous journey. After four days they reached 18,000 feet (5,486 meters) and set up camp. Continuing up the mountain, they established eight more camps. From the ninth camp, Hillary and Tenzing began the final ascent. Once the two mountaineers reached the top of the world, they took photographs, buried small items in the snow, and took some time to enjoy the view. After only 15 minutes, they started the descent to the bottom of the mountain. Back in London, they were given a hero's welcome.

Since 1953 Mount Everest has been climbed many times, some using different routes to get to the top. Not all expeditions have been successful, and many climbers have died in their attempts to reach the summit.

Suggested Activities

Reading Read an account of the journey to the top of Mount Everest. One excellent resource is *Hillary and Tenzing Climb Everest* by Bob Davidson (Dillon Press, 1993). Stunning pictures accompany a text which makes the reader feel part of the expedition.

Terms Brainstorm some climbing terms on the board and define each one. Discuss the terms as they apply to mountain climbing. Some words to include are *altitude sickness, crevasse, acclimatize, avalanche, reconnaissance*, and *traverse*.

Record Book Start a class *Mount Everest Record Book*. Record interesting facts, such as the first European woman to reach the summit, the first person to climb Mount Everest without using oxygen, and the expedition with the worst fatality record.

China Annexes Tibet

After the Communists took over China in 1949, they invaded the strategic border area of Tibet. In 1950 the defeated Tibet was forced to sign a treaty making it part of China. Resentment brewed in Tibet until 1959 when an uprising occurred. The rebellion was crushed by Chinese forces, and the Dalai Lama, the Tibetan religious leader, fled to India along with many of his followers. In 1965 Tibet was officially instituted as an autonomous region of China and since 1980 has been governed by a people's government whose leader heads the Tibetan Communist party.

Learn more about the land and people of Tibet. Fill in the blanks with the correct words. Choose words from the box below and use context clues to help you.

elevation	Nepal
temperatures	Mt. McKinley
scales	climate
Mt. Everest	inhabitants
Himalayas	Indus
snow	China
Po	plateau
mountains	area
monsoons	rain
Japan	Pyrenees

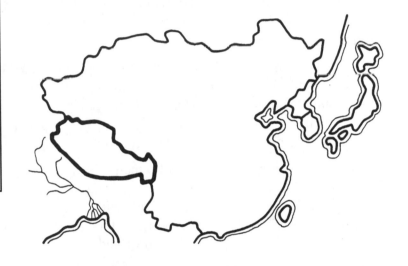

Tibet forms the southwest part of 1. _____ . Its 2. _____ encompasses 471,700 square miles or 1,221,700 square kilometers and is home to approximately 2,300,000 3. _____ . The 4. _____ form its southern boundaries with India, 5. _____ , Bhutan, Burma, and Pakistan. Much of Tibet's geography consists of the largest and highest 6. _____ on Earth. Its average 7. _____ is 15,000 feet or 4,600 meters.

8. _____ surround Tibet—the Kunluns are to the north, and the Himalayas are in the south. The world's highest peaks, including 9. _____ , can be found in the Himalayas. These mountains are the source of the great rivers of east and south Asia, including the 10. _____ .

Tibet's 11. _____ varies little with the seasons—12. _____ range from 45° F to 18° F. Because mountains block the 13. _____ , Tibet receives only 10 inches or 255 mm of 14. _____ annually.

Civil War in Vietnam

The war in Vietnam, which played a major role in the United States in the sixties, did not begin in the sixties as some might think, and the situation did not start out with United States involvement. Here are the facts about the origin of the Vietnam war.

Background After the Japanese were defeated in World War II, Ho Chi Minh declared the independence of all of Vietnam and established the Democratic Republic of Vietnam with Hanoi as the capital. Emperor Bao Dai abdicated his throne. In 1946, France attempted to reclaim its former colonies in Indochina, which included Cambodia, Laos, and Vietnam. The French created a new state of Vietnam in the south and a new capital, Saigon, and restored Bao Dai to the throne in 1949. American President Harry S. Truman recognized the new state in 1950 and sent American military personnel to train Vietnamese soldiers. The Vietnamese communists, also known as the Viet Minh, continued to attack the French.

Action In November of 1953, French paratroopers were dropped over northwest Vietnam and captured Dien Bien Phu. French military leaders thought that the Vietnamese guerrillas would come down from the mountains and be easy targets. But the leader of the Viet Minh, General Giap, had led a huge army to the outskirts of Dien Bien Phu before the paratroopers arrived. Twenty thousand men with equipment on bicycles followed the soldiers who dragged field guns over the mountains.

Seige The French garrison of 19,000 men was completely surrounded by the Viet Minh. For 55 days the two sides battled it out, but at the beginning of May 1954 the French surrendered. Since they did not hold any of the territory around Dien Bien Phu, there was no place left for them to go. France asked the United States to send troops. Although the United States recognized the Saigon government, President Eisenhower refused to get involved.

Cost Since 1946 the fight in Vietnam had cost the French 95,000 soldiers and eleven billion dollars. The fall of Dien Bien Phu finally convinced the French to give up. The United States had backed the French financially, providing up to 80 percent of the cost of the war.

UN Ruling On July 21, 1954, the French and Viet Minh agreed to a cease fire. The United Nations ruled that Vietnam should be divided into two countries along the seventeenth parallel until reunification elections were held within two years. In October of 1954 thousands of refugees left North Vietnam for South Vietnam. President Eisenhower sent American ships to transport them. In 1955 Emperor Bao Dai was deposed, South Vietnam was declared a republic, and Ngo Dinh Diem became the first president of South Vietnam. (Election returns showed that Diem received more votes than there were registered voters.) France agreed to support this government, and the United States offered direct economic and military aid to South Vietnam.

Aftermath Ngo Dinh Diem refused to hold the reunification election, stating that the people of North Vietnam were not free to express their true wishes.

Suggested Activities

Mapping Draw and label a map of 1954 Vietnam. Include the following: China, Thailand, Cambodia, Laos, North Vietnam, the 17th parallel, South Vietnam, Hanoi, Dien Bien Phu, Saigon, and the South China Sea.

Theory President Eisenhower did not want to see a communist government in North Vietnam because he was afraid that any communist gains in Southeast Asia would lead to a "domino effect." In pairs, establish a definition of Eisenhower's Domino Theory.

The ANZUS Treaty

Australia and New Zealand had fought together during World War I, and in World War II they had joined forces with Britain and the United States. In the years following World War II, Australia and the U.S. strengthened the close relationship they had developed during their wartime cooperation. On September 1, 1951, Australia, New Zealand, and the United States signed a mutual defense agreement called the ANZUS Treaty.

The name ANZUS is an acronym formed by the initial letters of the three countries: Australia, New Zealand, and the United States. Below are some other historical acronyms with which you should be familiar. Write the number of the acronym on the line next to the correct description.

Acronym		**Description**
1. NATO	_____	A. A line of radar installations built across the Arctic
2. OAU	_____	B. Disarmament and arms limitations talks
3. USSR	_____	C. United Nations agency that specializes in child welfare
4. UNESCO	_____	D. Organization that works for civil rights for black Americans
5. DEW	_____	E. Treaty signed by European countries and the United States to defend against agressions from the Soviet Union
6. UNICEF	_____	F. Before its breakup, it was the largest country in the world
7. SEATO	_____	G. The UN agency that helps develop education in poor countries
8. WHO	_____	H. Thirty African states formed this union in 1963
9. SALT	_____	I. The UN agency that advises countries on health services
10. NAACP	_____	J. A defense treaty signed after the French left Indochina in 1954

On the lines below identify the whole name of each acronym.

1. NATO _____
2. OAU _____
3. USSR _____
4. UNESCO_____
5. DEW _____

6. UNICEF _____
7. SEATO _____
8. WHO_____
9. SALT_____
10. NAACP _____

Answers: (fold under before copying)

1.E 2.H 3.F 4.G 5.A 6.C 7.J 8.I 9.B 10.D

1.North Atlantic Treaty Organization 2.Organization of African Unity 3.Union of Soviet Socialist Republics 4.United Nations Educational, Scientific, and Cultural Organization 5.Distant Early Warning 6.United Nations Children's Fund 7.Southeast Asia Treaty Organization 8.World Health Organization 9.Strategic Arms Limitation Talks 10.National Association for the Advancement of Colored People

Protesting Communism

Throughout the fifties people in communist-occupied countries became increasingly disenchanted with the system of government. Read about two major incidents in Europe during this period.

The East Berlin Uprising

In 1949 East Berlin had become the capital of the Soviet satellite state of East Germany. People there had grown increasingly unhappy with the Soviet occupation. During June of 1953, the East Germans went on strike to protest the government's demand for higher production quotas. Workers were being forced to work longer hours but this was not their only complaint. They were also dissatisfied with their low standard of living and the fact that thousands of German prisoners of war were still in Russia. When the government did not respond to the strike, workers began to riot and tear down Communist flags in the city. Soviet troops and tanks responded quickly and fired on the crowds of angry workers, killing hundreds in the melee. It was a savage response which showed the East Berliners that dissent would not be tolerated behind the Iron Curtain. This demonstration marked the first time that anyone had openly rebelled against a Communist state. It would not be the last.

Suggested Activity

Research Tell students to conduct research and find answers to these questions: What is the Iron Curtain? Does it still exist today?

Hungary's Fight for Freedom

Following World War II the Soviet Union controlled Hungary. Russian secret police spied on Hungarians, and no one was allowed freedom of speech. On February 25, 1956, Soviet Premier Nikita Khrushchev attacked and denounced Joseph Stalin, the former leader of the Soviet Union. Soon after that students in Budapest, Hungary, staged a huge demonstration to protest the Soviet domination of their country. They destroyed a huge bronze statue of Stalin in the city center and demanded that all Russian troops leave Hungary. The Hungarian army entered into the fray and helped former premier Imre Nagy return to power (Nagy had been ousted by the Soviets in 1955). After Nagy announced Hungary's withdrawal from the Warsaw Pact, the Soviets bombed the center of Budapest, and one thousand tanks flattened civilian houses. The Hungarians did not have the manpower or weapons to resist the Soviet attack. Some 200,000 refugees fled across the border into Yugoslavia and Austria but paid heavy prices to have professional guides lead them to safety.

Suggested Activities

Mapping Work in pairs. On a map of Europe locate Hungary, Yugoslavia, and Austria. Plot the best routes from Budapest to both Yugoslavia and Austria.

Pact Research the Warsaw Pact and write a paragraph explaining who signed it and what its provisions were. Discuss.

Matisse

One of the most important artists of the 20th century is Frenchman Henri Matisse. Born in 1869, he led an art movement called post-Impressionism and was one of the first famous collage artists. Throughout his productive and prolific career, Matisse's style continued to evolve as he experimented with different colors, art forms, and mediums.

When Matisse was growing up, he did not have dreams of becoming a famous artist, but a quirk of fate led him to that new career. While training to become a lawyer, he had to have surgery. During his recuperation, his mother bought him some paints and a how-to book. From then on Matisse was totally devoted to art. His bourgeois father took a dim view of his son's new career path, and as Matisse was leaving for Paris, his father yelled out, "You'll starve!"

After one year at the Academie Julian, Matisse went on to study at the Academie Carriere. Throughout these early years he copied the Impressionistic style of painting and the Japanese style of woodblock prints. As Matisse came in contact with other styles, his work gradually changed.

In 1904 Matisse had his first one-man show which met with little success. By the following year, he was the leader of the Fauvist movement which relied on bright colors and distorted shapes. Critics were shocked by the new forms and called it the work of wild beasts, or *Fauvism* in French. While the actual movement lasted only a few years, its effects on the art world have been felt ever since.

In addition to painting, Matisse opened his own art academy for children in 1908. That same year, he published *Notes of a Painter* in which he expressed his artistic beliefs. Later, he executed murals, created stage designs for a ballet, drew several series of book illustrations, and made sculptures and collages. Those collages were some of the most important pieces of work that he ever produced. Even more impressive is the fact that he created many of them when he was in his eighties and sick in bed. He would instruct his assistants to paint huge pieces of paper with bright colors. Then he would cut out the shapes. As directed, the assistants pinned the shapes onto white paper and then pasted them down.

A master of color, Henri Matisse brought a special joyfulness and a childlike perspective to his art. When Matisse died in 1954, he left a part of himself behind for all future generations to enjoy.

Suggested Activities

Collage In small groups, create giant collages. See the instructions in the text above.

Extensions For additional activities on Matisse, see *Teacher Created Materials #494 Focus on Artists.*

First-Person Story Starters

Provide a copy of the following story starters for each individual or pair of students. Direct them to read through the list and choose one that interests them. Have them cut out the strip they have chosen and glue it to the top of a sheet of paper. Tell them to complete the story.

1. I am famed artist Henri Matisse. My ill health keeps me confined to bed, but that will not prevent me from creating a work of art. With the help of my assistants I will make a huge collage. First,. . .

2. They say there are 60,000 fans in this Stockholm stadium waiting for their team to win its first World Cup. I want to help my team to win the honor. Sure, I am only 17, and my knee still hurts since the injury, but . . .

3. It is difficult for me to believe that I am actually at the top of Mt. Everest. It has been such a long, hard journey. Norgay and I are the first to reach this point on Earth. What tales I will have for my grandchildren . . .

4. Welcome to Antarctica. I am a glaciologist and am part of a team of scientists who are studying the area. My scientific inquiries concern the continental ice shelf, glaciers, and past climates of the continent. My work . . .

5. This newspaper article says that I, Mary Leakey, discovered the Zinjanthropus man, nicknamed the Nutcracker Man. A hominid (man-ape) fossil, it is believed to be 1,750,000 years old. This is how my discovery came about . . .

6. My name is Emil Zatopek, and I am a Czechoslovakian military officer. My first race here at the Helsinki Olympics was easy to win. Surely I can run a marathon. What does it matter that I have never run a marathon before?

7. I am Laika, a female Samoyed, and I have been chosen to become the first animal in space. In a few days I will be placed inside *Sputnik II* and launched into orbit. It sounds very exciting, but I do have some concerns . . .

8. For some time now my comrades and I have been unhappy with the Soviet occupation. Then last evening at the end of my shift, it was announced that we would have to work long hours to meet higher production quotas. It will do me no good because. . .

9. My name is Tony Sailer, and I am a downhill skier for Austria. I have been chosen to be on my country's 1956 Olympics team. Although I have never been to Cortina, Italy, I am confident that all of my practicing will. . .

10. The news is not good. Last night our leader, Nasser, nationalized the Suez Canal. He wants to use the canal tolls to pay for construction of the Aswan Dam. I think it is a fine idea but the British are quite upset, and I fear that. . .

Fifties Facts and Figures

Make a copy of the chart below for each pair of students. Direct them to use the information on this page as a comparison with a chart which they will complete about the current decade. Discuss the similarities and the differences between the fifties and the current decade.

The United States in the Fifties

Population:	150,697,999
National Debt:	$256 billion
Federal Minimum Wage:	75 cents per hour (raised to $1 per hour in 1955)
Postage:	raised from 3 cents to 4 cents in 1958
Popular Books:	*Profiles in Courage, On the Road, Lord of the Flies, The Lord of the Rings, The Spirit of St. Louis, The Old Man and the Sea, East of Eden, The Catcher in the Rye, The Sea Around Us, Atlas Shrugged, Dr. Zhivago, Hawaii, Goldfinger, Portnoy's Complaint*
Popular Movies:	*Ben Hur, High Noon, The Greatest Show on Earth, Roman Holiday, From Here to Eternity, On the Waterfront, Rear Window, Marty, The Seven Year Itch, Around the World in 80 Days, The Ten Commandments, The King and I, The Man with the Golden Arm, The Bridge on the River Kwai*
Popular Stars:	Brigette Bardot, Grace Kelly, Natalie Wood, Audrey Hepburn, Deborah Kerr, Elizabeth Taylor, Debbie Reynolds, Marilyn Monroe, Charlton Heston, Gary Cooper, John Wayne, Marlon Brando, Yul Brynner, James Dean, Jimmy Stewart, Jack Lemmon, Paul Newman, Sidney Poitier, Glenn Ford, Laurence Olivier, Gene Kelly, William Holden, David Niven
Popular Songs:	"A Bushel and a Peck," "Good Night, Irene," "C'est Si Bon," "Your Cheatin' Heart," "I Saw Mommy Kissing Santa Claus," "Doggie in the Window," "Mr. Sandman," "The Yellow Rose of Texas," "Davy Crockett," "Sixteen Tons," "Mack the Knife," "Chipmunk Song," "The Purple People Eater," "Catch a Falling Star," "Maria," "Seventy-Six Trombones," "Tom Dooley," "He's Got the Whole World in His Hands," "Rock Around the Clock," "Charlie Brown," "Poison Ivy," "Sixteen Candles"
Popular TV Shows:	*What's My Line?, Father Knows Best, The Ozzie and Harriet Show, Leave It to Beaver, I Love Lucy, Amos 'n' Andy, The Ed Sullivan Show, Milton Berle, The George Burns and Gracie Allen Show, Dragnet, American Bandstand, Gunsmoke, Wagon Train, Roy Rogers, Hopalong Cassidy, The Howdy Doody Show, Captain Kangaroo, Lassie, Kukla, Fran and Ollie, Mickey Mouse Club, Rin Tin Tin, Captain Midnight*
Fashions:	pink shirts for males, chemise dresses for females, poodle skirts, ponytails and bouffant hairdos; ducktails and crewcuts, jeans, t-shirts, and leather jackets for males
Fads:	Hula-Hoops, 3-D movies, Davy Crockett hats, goldfish swallowing, crowding into sports cars, stuffing people into telephone booths, dancing the cha-cha
Popular Toys:	Hula-Hoops, Frisbees, Barbie dolls, Scrabble, paint-by-number sets

Then and Now Worksheet

With your partner fill in the blanks on this page. Compare your answers with the Fifties Facts and Figures on page 81.

U.S. Now _____
(year)

Population _____

National Debt _____

Federal Minimum Wage _____

United States Postage _____

Popular Books _____

_____

Popular Movies _____

_____

Popular Stars _____

_____

Popular Songs _____

_____

Popular TV Shows _____

_____

Fashions _____

_____

Fads _____

_____

Popular Cars _____

_____

Popular Toys _____

Fads and Fashions Crossword

See how well you know the clothing and crazes of the fifties. All of the clues on the crossword puzzle below are about the fads and fashions of the fifties.

Across

2. This term describes slim pants that reached to the calves.

4. This is the name given to the decade's new music craze.

5. These are now called jeans.

7. It made professional sports popular.

8. Worn under full skirts, this garment is made of nylon netting

9. This describes a series of quick hand movements done to rock and roll music.

10. This frozen meal served in an aluminum tray was introduced in the 1950s.

11. An outdoor movie theater, this was a popular spot in the fifties.

13. This is a favorite meeting place for Beatniks

Down

1. Alfred E. Newman was the mascot of this zany comic.

3. This was the favorite footwear of teenage girls.

6. This term was used for nonconformists of the fifties.

12. This name was given to slim skirts.

14. This plastic disk is thrown to a partner.

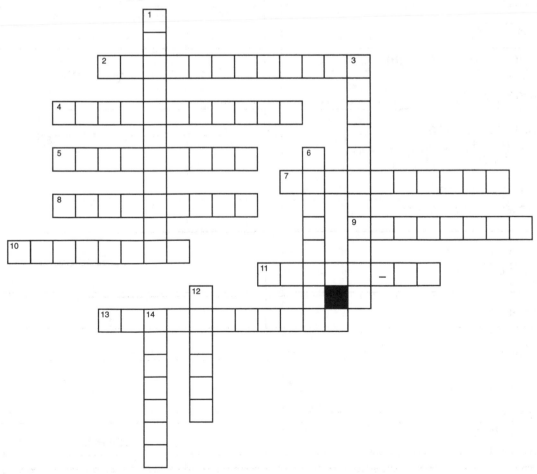

Fifties Personalities Game

Students can test their knowledge of important people of the fifties with this game. Give each pair of students a copy of this page. Direct them to cut out the rectangles, keeping the Clue Cards separate from the Personality Cards. Instruct them to choose a Clue Card and read the clue. Match it with the correct Personality Card. Continue in the same manner until all the cards have been matched.

Clue Cards	Personality Cards
blue-suede shoes king of rock and roll	Jack Kerouac
architect Guggenheim Museum	Walt Disney
red hair *"I Love Lucy"*	Rosa Parks
source of "Red Scare" senator	Julius and Ethel Rosenberg
The Cat in the Hat Theodore S. Geisel	Leonard Bernstein
head of NAACP Legal Defense Fund segregation cases	Dr. Jonas Salk
composer & conductor director of N.Y. Philharmonic	Thurgood Marshall
Magic Kingdom *Mickey Mouse Club*	Frank Lloyd Wright
the Beat Generation *On the Road*	Elvis Presley
accused of espionage sentenced to electric chair	Dr. Seuss
polio dead-virus vaccine	Joseph McCarthy
seamstress Montgomery bus boycott	Lucille Ball

Fifties-Style Math

All of the problems on this page are based on inventions and events of the 1950s. Students can review math skills while learning some interesting facts about the era.

1. There were only 17,000 television sets in the United States in 1948, but by the end of the 1950s there were 50 million. How many more television sets were there in the late fifties than in 1948?

2. The GNP (Gross National Product) rose from $318 billion in 1950 to $503 billion in 1960. On the average, how much did the GNP rise each year during this ten-year period?

3. Altogether, the United States suffered 157,000 deaths and injuries during the Korean War. Of that number 54,000 died. How many were injured?

4. In 1867 Russia sold Alaska to the United States for $7 million dollars, or 2 cents an acre. How many acres did Alaska contain altogether?

5. British athlete Roger Bannister ran a mile in just under four minutes. His time was 3 minutes, 59.4 seconds. At that rate, how far could he run in one hour?

6. Between the years 1942 and 1950, 39 million "war babies" were born. On the average, how many war babies were born each year during this period?

7. Twelve-year-old George Wright III won $100,000 on the TV quiz show *The Big Surprise* in 1956. After taxes, he had $40,000 for his own. How much did he pay in taxes?

8. The 1950 census said that New York state led the nation in population. Manhattan alone had 1,938,551 people in its 22 square miles. Approximately how many people lived in each square mile?

9. In 1955 Dick and Mac's original McDonald's boasted that they had sold over one million burgers. At that time a hamburger sold for 15 cents. How much money did the first one million burgers bring in for the company?

10. To ease the housing shortage after World War II, Levittown houses were developed. At one point, 36 such homes could be completed in a day. How many could be constructed in 14 days?

11. By 1958 singer Elvis Presley had sold 40 million records in two years. At that rate, how many records could he have been expected to sell in seven years?

12. When the Hula-Hoop debuted in 1958, they cost $1.98 each. In the first six months, 20 million of the toys had been sold. How much did they cost altogether?

What Year Was That?

Check how well you remember the events of the fifties with this quiz. After each number read the three clues given. Decide in what year all three events occurred and circle the year of your answer.

1. *Sputnik I* is launched. A Civil Rights Act is passed. The first Dr. Seuss book is published.

           1955   1956   1957

2. The 22nd Amendment is passed. The Rosenbergs are executed. *I Love Lucy* premieres on television.

           1951   1952   1953

3. Alaska becomes the 49th state. The Guggenheim Museum opens. The Antarctic treaty is signed by 12 nations.

           1957   1958   1959

4. The first 3-D movies are shown in theaters. Dwight D. Eisenhower is elected president. Puerto Rico becomes the first United States commonwealth.

           1951   1952   1953

5. The Korean War ends. Color television telecasts begin. Jackie Cochran becomes the first woman to break the sound barrier.

           1952   1953   1954

6. The Federal Highway Act provides funding for interstate roads. The Suez crisis ends. Crest, the first fluoride toothpaste, is introduced.

           1954   1955   1956

7. The *Peanuts* comic strip is first published. The Korean War begins. The first kidney transplant surgery is performed.

           1950   1951   1952

8. The Holiday Inn hotel chain is founded. *Mad Magazine* goes on sale. The first hydrogen bomb is exploded.

           1951   1952   1953

9. The first rock and roll song makes the charts. The Montgomery bus boycott begins. Disneyland opens in Anaheim, California.

           1955   1956   1957

10. The Vietnam war begins. Laika becomes the first animal in space. United States troops are sent to Little Rock to enforce integration.

            1956   1957   1958

11. Hula-Hoops make their debut. NASA is founded. The microchip is invented.

            1956   1957   1958

12. The Putt Putt golf course is invented. The United States Navy launches the first nuclear-powered sub, *Nautilus*. Elvis Presley makes his first record.

            1953   1954   1955

The Rebellious Sixties

The fifties decade was a prosperous, mostly uneventful time in American history. Jobs were plentiful and people had money to spend. Consumer goods were now available and plentiful. Almost every home boasted a television set and many had at least one car. Life was good during these times.

With the election of John F. Kennedy, Americans were inspired to devote themselves to the cause of social justice. During his 1961 inaugural speech he implored Americans to "Ask not what your country can do for you, ask what you can do for your country." Young and old alike were eager to lend a helping hand in a number of causes. Many joined the Peace Corps, while others devoted themselves to the fight for civil rights. Although legislation in the fifties provided for school integration, in the sixties attention focused on eliminating discrimination in public places and in employment opportunities. Throughout the sixties the issue of civil rights grew stronger. Powerful black leaders emerged, most notably Martin Luther King, Jr., and gathered their people to demonstrate against the injustices they had been enduring. They waged their campaign with non-violent means, like sit-ins and marches, and often met with beatings, bombings, and even shootings. As the decade progressed, many were discouraged and frustrated by the slow pace of nonviolent change, and blacks turned to new leaders who advocated "Black power." Riots in urban areas followed. When Martin Luther King was assassinated in 1968, there were race riots in 124 cities.

New forms of music and entertainment reflected the serious attitude of young people. Folk singers with acoustic guitars sang traditional ballads. A new group of folk artists, including Bob Dylan, Joan Baez, and Phil Ochs wrote songs about current social problems.

When Kennedy was assassinated before the completion of his first term, the nation was shocked and saddened. The new president, Lyndon Baines Johnson, declared a "war on poverty" and began his administration with the passage of several measures in his Great Society program, including Medicare, Medicaid, Operation Headstart, and a civil rights act.

Attention focused on the Southeast Asian nation of Vietnam where the role of American troops had changed from that of advisors to full-blown war. United States troops were helping the South Vietnamese in their civil war against the Communist North Vietnamese, but not everyone supported this idea. As more and more soldiers were brought home in body bags, people took notice and began protesting in ever-increasing numbers. For the first time, events in the war were televised as they happened, bringing the horror of war into the public's living rooms. Some young men fled to Canada and other parts of the world rather than face the draft. Others burned their draft cards and found ways to avoid serving in the military.

Protest was a way of life in the sixties. Women eventually joined the ranks of protestors. No longer content to be suburban housewives, they wanted the same career opportunities and choices afforded to men. Betty Friedan led the women's liberation movement and formed the National Organization of Women. Migrant workers united under the leadership of Cesar Chavez and protested the unsafe, low-paying conditions of their labor. Young people rejected both the culture and politics of their elders. Many joined the counterculture, which advocated peace and love.

Literature Connections

One surefire way to interest students in a specific topic is through the use of children's literature. Read through the annotated bibliographies to decide which pieces of literature you might like to use with your class. Helpful suggestions for extending the books follow each description.

The Gold Cadillac by Mildred D. Taylor (Dial, 1987)

Summary: When Daddy drives home in a brand new Cadillac, everyone is impressed except Mama. She steadfastly refuses to ride in it until Daddy decides to take the car on a trip south to Mississippi. Mama insists on accompanying him, and the whole family forms a caravan. As they get closer to their destination they see signs reading "Whites only" and "Colored not allowed." Then Daddy is stopped by the police and accused of stealing the car. Wilma and her sister find out for the first time what it is like to be afraid because of the color of their skin. This story paints an unforgettable picture of growing up black in America during the 1950s.

Extensions

Discussion Questions Assess students' comprehension and understanding with some discussion questions. For example, why were people impressed with the Cadillac? What did the family members have to say when Daddy decided to drive the car to Mississippi to visit their grandparents? Why did the police arrest Daddy? What made Mama change her mind about the car? Why did Daddy sell the Cadillac?

Mapping Reread page 27 and take note of the route they drove. Draw a map and label all the cities and states mentioned on that page. On a map measure the distances from Toledo to each of those cities.

Response Write the following statement on the board. Instruct the students to respond in writing. "As fine as the Cadillac had been," he said, "it had pulled us apart for a while." Discuss the responses in whole group.

Comparisons Compare the family's life in Toledo, Ohio, with the treatment they received in Mississippi. Are conditions in the South today the same or better than they were in the fifties?

Further Reading If students enjoyed this book, they will also like to read other titles by Mildred Taylor including *Let the Circle Be Unbroken, Roll of Thunder Hear My Cry,* and *Song of the Trees* (all published by Dial).

Youn Hee and Me by C. S. Adler (Harcourt Brace & Company, 1995)

Summary: Caitlin and her mom are surprised to learn that Simon has a sister still living in an orphanage in Korea. Without hesitation, they decide to try to adopt her. Living with Youn Hee turns out to be far different from what they had imagined. For one thing, Youn Hee speaks very little English, and she disapproves of the way Simon is being disciplined. Each girl feels that her position as Simon's sister is being challenged, but they manage to work through their problems and differences. In the process they learn about each other's culture and become a real family. Although it has a contemporary setting, this is a great book to use when studying the Korean War.

Extensions

Concerns Caitlin's mom had some reservations about adding Youn Hee to their family. What were some of her concerns? How did Caitlin answer them? Have the students speculate about what concerns Youn Hee may have had about joining an American family.

Literature Connections *(cont.)*

Dictionary Begin a class Korean-English dictionary. As Korean words and phrases are encountered within the text, write each one on a separate index card along with its English translation. Place the cards in an index box.

Role Play Pair the students. One plays Caitlin, the other Youn Hee who has just arrived from Korea. Have Caitlin instruct Youn Hee how to use the microwave or television. Let the students exchange roles.

Culture Increase understanding by exploring Korean culture. See page 29 for a list of activities.

Christmas Direct the students to draw some traditional Christmas symbols. Tell them to research and draw symbols of a traditional Korean Christmas celebration. Have them describe some of the Christmas traditions that are observed there. Learn about some of the other holidays, including their Lunar New Year and how birthdays are celebrated.

Respond Write the following statement on the board and discuss it with the class or have them respond in writing. "We can't be sisters, Caitlin. I'm Korean and you're not."

Relationships. Draw a large triangle on the board. Label each point with a different name: Caitlin, Simon, Youn Hee. Have students describe the relationships among the characters. Write the information on the lines between characters' names. If preferred, pairs of students could complete a triangular relationship graphic.

Empathy Tell the students to put themselves in Youn Hee's place. Discuss what they would miss the most about their homeland if they were suddenly moved to a new country. What difficulties and challenges would they probably face?

. . . If You Lived at the Time of Martin Luther King by Ellen Levine (Scholastic, Inc., 1990).

Summary Your class can learn all about the civil rights movement and the life and times of Martin Luther King, Jr. with this book. It is written in a question-and-answer format and provides answers to some of the most-asked questions about the civil rights era.

Extensions

Warm Up Before introducing the book *. . . If You Lived at the Time of Martin Luther King* to the class, write the term civil rights on the board. Ask the class to brainstorm a list of questions they have about this period in American history. Record the students' questions and post them on the chalkboard for all to see.

Answers Assign a number of questions from the brainstorming session to each group. Direct them to find and write answers to the questions, using *. . . If You Lived at the Time of Martin Luther King* as a resource.

Protest Songs The words and music to one of the best-known protest songs, "We Shall Overcome," are provided on the back page of this book. Find out the names of some other popular protest songs. Practice singing them or listen to recordings.

Venn Diagram With the whole class discuss segregation in the North versus segregation in the South during the fifties. Group the students and have them prepare a Venn diagram to show the similarities and differences in segregation in the two geographic areas of the United States.

Comparisons Assign the students to write a one-page report comparing Malcolm X's views on integration with Martin Luther King, Jr.'s. Tell the students to include Malcolm X's views while he was a member of the Black Muslims and after he left the religious group. A fine resource to use is *Malcolm X: Black Rage* by David R. Collins (Dillon, 1994).

Cooperative Stories

Work with four other classmates to write a cooperative fifties story. Here's how: First, determine the order in which each member will participate. Now, the first member of your group will write a sentence that incorporates the first phrase below. Next, the second group member writes a sentence using the second phrase below. Keep going until five sentences have been completed. Then conduct a group brainstorming session and discuss ways to tie all the sentences together into one creative fifties story. It can be as funny or as serious as you want to make it. Write your completed story on the back of this page. Share it with the rest of the class.

Topic	Sentence
1. five red and white striped Hula-Hoops	
2. an unopened jar of crunchy Jif peanut butter	
3. four pairs of 3-D glasses	
4. lime green glow-in-the-dark plastic Frisbees	
5. a pony-tailed Barbie in her blue evening gown	

90

A Feel for the Fifties

On this page you will find some suggested ways to motivate creative writing. All are based on 1950s events and were designed to help students get a feel for the times.

Beat Poets Read some poems aloud to the class (see *Beat Voices* edited by David Kherdian, Henry Holt and Company, 1995; preview the poems as some of them contain explicit language). Ask the students to write their own beat poems. Place a stool in front of the room and let students take turns sitting on it while they share their poems. If possible, have someone softly play bongo drums in the background. Serve "coffee" (hot cocoa or tea) to the class to create a beatnik coffeehouse atmosphere. Have the audience applaud by snapping their fingers.

TV Families Record a typical 1950s family sit-com such as *Leave It to Beaver* or *Father Knows Best*. After discussing the show, divide the students into small groups. Direct them to write a script for an episode of that program. Remind them to keep in mind the way people talked, what conveniences were invented then, and how children behaved toward their parents and elders.

Fairy Tales Read aloud a Korean fairy tale, *The Korean Cinderella* by Shirley Climo (or the Disney version). Direct the students to write a modern version of the Cinderella story.

Dr. Seuss In 1957 Dr. Seuss published his first book, *The Cat in the Hat*. Group the students and tell them to read the story. As they do so, have them make a list of all the words used in the text. Direct the groups to write a children's story using only the words that appear in *The Cat in the Hat*. Let them share their stories with the whole class.

Charge It When company executive Frank McNamara finished a business meeting and realized he had left his cash at home, he persuaded the restaurant owner to wait for payment. To prevent such a recurrence, he worked with a bank to introduce the first multipurpose charge card on February 28, 1950–the Diners Club card. Today, credit cards are used for all kinds of purchases. Write a creative story in which paper money is no longer in existence and people make all their purchases with plastic cards.

Mistake Out Bette Nesmith Graham was an executive secretary who made plenty of typing errors. To correct her mistakes she mixed some tempera paint with a few other ingredients and carefully fixed her flubs. So many secretaries were borrowing her invention that she decided to market her Mistake Out (now marketed as Liquid Paper). Pretend you are Ms. Graham. Write a speech that will convince the executives at IBM that this will be a worthwhile venture.

Cha Cha In 1958 the cha cha became a popular dance. Pretend you are the dance teacher. Write the instructions you would give your pupils as you teach them the steps to this dance.

Cold War The cold war following World War II led to an arms race between America and the USSR. As more and more nuclear weapons were developed, people became increasingly concerned about and aware of radiation dangers. Many prepared for a possible attack by building fallout shelters. Group the students and ask them to brainstorm a list of things that would be needed for survival in a fallout shelter. Have each student select one item from the list and write a paragraph explaining its importance for survival. If desired, have each student decided what one personal thing he or she would include in the shelter. Ask them to write a paragraph describing the item, and its significance, in detail.

New to the Fifties

New inventions, habits, lifestyles, and occupations cause people to invent new words. The 1950s were no exception. Listed below are some of the words and phrases that came into popular use throughout the decade.

Beat Jack Kerouac coined this word to describe his generation. It means both beatific, or blessed, and defeated. Those who took up the Beat lifestyle believed they were blessed with spiritual powers and misundersood by society.

Beat Generation This name is given to those who rebelled against social conventions, experimented with drugs, spoke their own slang language, and wore clothes different from mainstream America in the 1950s.

Beatniks Individuals who followed the Beat lifestyle were called beatniks.

boycott This term means there is an organized agreement in which a group refuses to have anything to do with another group, company, or organization until certain conditions have been met.

Cold War This refers to a period of tension and hostility between the United States and the USSR that stopped short of war.

cool This is a slang term for good.

crazy This slang term means great.

desegregation This word means to integrate or to abolish racial segregation.

dig In 1950s slang, this meant to like, as in "She digs Elvis."

discrimination Prejudice against another person or group, usually because of race or religion, is discrimination.

Edsel After this Ford model debuted in 1957 and failed to sell, the name became synonymous with error or failure.

Indochina This is an area of Southeast Asia that includes the countries of Laos, Cambodia, and Vietnam.

McCarthyism This term means charges made without proof and accompanied by publicity.

orbit The path that a spacecraft or other heavenly body makes as it revolves around another body is its orbit. For example, *Sputnik* orbited the earth.

Palestine This is the name given by the Arabs to Israel, a country at the eastern end of the Mediterranean.

pad This slang term was used by Beatniks to refer to an apartment.

segregation This term refers to the forced separation of one group from others. For example, some schools, buses, and bathrooms were segregated and marked "for colored only" or "whites only".

Soviet Union This is a shortened version of the Union of Soviet Socialist Republics (USSR), the official name for Russia in the postwar years.

Sputnik This word means fellow traveler in Russian. It was the name of the first unmanned space satellite.

square This slang term was used to refer to someone considered dull or unattractive.

Suggested Activities

Creative Writing Choose one word from the list above and write a creative story explaining how that word came into popular use during the 1950s.

Slang In small groups, make a list of the slang terms from the list above. Determine if those slang words are still in use today or what words have replaced them.

Say What?

Beatniks and teens of the fifties had a language all their own. Read each slang statement below. Translate it on the lines provided. A list of definitions at the bottom of the page will help you interpret meanings.

1. The *cat flipped* over the new *chick* in school.

   _____

2. That was one *hairy* math test!

   _____

3. He drives a *bomb* with *snowballs*.

   _____

4. She thinks that song will be a *dog*.

   _____

5. I need some *bread* to take my girl to the *passion pit* tonight.

   _____

6. She's going out with a real *cool cat*.

   _____

7. When he asked me for the test answers, I told him to *blast off*.

   _____

8. That *square* keeps trying to hang around our group.

   _____

In the space below write a sentence of your own using any of the slang words in the Definitions Box below.

_____

_____

Definitions Box

blast off—go away; get lost
bomb—an old car
bread—money
cat—any man
chick—girl
cool—neat; groovy
crazy—wonderful; great
dog—song that did not make it to hit status

flip—become enthusiastic
hairy—tough; difficult
hip—someone who is aware and with it
passion pit—a drive-in movie
snowballs—whitewall tires
square—a dull person; an outsider
wheels—a car

Software in the Classroom

More and more software is finding its way into the classroom. Many of the multimedia packages allow students to access photos, speeches, film clips, maps, and newspapers of various eras in history. Although a program may not be written specifically for the topic you are studying, existing software may be adapted for your purposes. To get maximum use from these programs and to learn how to keep up with technology, try some of the suggestions below.

Software

American Heritage: The History of the United States For Young People. Byron Preiss Multimedia

American History CD. Multi-Educator

Compton's Encyclopedia of American History. McGraw Hill

The Chronicle. Sunburst Communications

Compton's Interactive Encyclopedia Compton's New Media, Inc.

The Cruncher. Microsoft Works

Encarta (various editions). Microsoft Home

Ideas That Changed the World. Ice Publishing

Our Times: Multimedia Encyclopedia of the 20th Century (Vicarious Point of View Series 2.0). Scholastic

Presidents: A Picture History of Our Nation. National Geographic

Time Almanac. Compact Publishing, available through Broderbund, 800-922-9204

TimeLiner from Tom Snyder Productions, 800-342-0236

Time Traveler CD! Orange Cherry

Vital Links. Educational Resources (includes videodisc and audio cassette)

Where in America's Past is Carmen Sandiego? Broderbund

Compton's Interactive Encyclopedia. Compton's New Media, Inc.

Using the Programs

After the initial excitement of using a new computer program wears off, you can still motivate students by letting them use the programs in different ways.

1. Print out a copy of a time line for 1950 for each group of students. Assign each group a different topic, e.g., entertainment, politics, etc. Direct the groups to research their topics and add text and pictures to their time lines.
2. Let each pair of students choose a specific photo from the 1950s. Have them research the event and write a news story to go with the picture.
3. Not enough computers? Hook your computer up to a TV screen for large-group activities or pair the students and let them take turns typing. Keep a kitchen timer handy. For more ideas see *Managing Technology in the Classroom* from Teacher Created Materials or the booklet *101+ Ways to Use a Computer in the Classroom* (Oxbow Creek Technology Committee, Oxbow Creek School, 6050 109th Ave. N., Champlin, MN 55316).

Internet

If you have access to the Internet, let the students search for related information. First ask the students to brainstorm a list of keywords or topics. Use a web browser like Alta Vista or Web Crawler to search for sites. Facts, picture and sound clips are only a click away. As an alternative, you may wish to preview sites and provide students with a list of URLs for access.

Note: If the students will be searching, you may wish to install a filtering program, like *SurfWatch* from Spyglass, to limit access to objectionable material. Check with your Internet Service Provider.

Keeping Current

To keep current with the ever-expanding list of available software programs, you may have to turn to a number of sources, including the ones below.

Magazines: *Instructor* and *Learning* (technology review columns and feature articles).

Children's Software Revue 520 North Adams Street Ypsilanti, Michigan 48197-2482. (Write for a free sample.)

PC Family and *PC Kids* (available at newsstands).

Books: *Great Teaching and the One-Computer Classroom* (Tom Snyder Productions, Inc., 800-342-0236).

Internet for Kids! by Ted Pederson and Francis Moss (Price Stern Sloan, Inc., 1995).

That's Edutainment! by Eric Brown (Osborne/McGraw, 1994).

Bibliography

Fiction

Note: All starred (*) titles were Newbery Award winners in the fifties.

*Clark, Ann Nolan. *Secret of the Andes.* Viking, 1953

Davis, Thulani. *1959: A Novel.* Grove Wiedenfeld, 1992.

*DeAngeli, Marguerite. *The Door in the Wall.* Doubleday, 1950.

*DeJong, Meindert. *The Wheel on the School.* Harper, 1955.

Duvoisin, Roger. *Petunia.* Knopf, 1950.

*Estes, Eleanor. *Ginger Pye.* Harcourt, 1952.

Herlihy, Dirlie. *Ludie's Song.* Dial, 1988.

*Keith, Harold. *Rifles for Watie.* Crowell, 1958.

*Krumgold, Joseph. *. . . And Now Miguel.* Crowell, 1954.

*Latham, Jean Lee. *Carry on, Mr. Bowditch.* Houghton, 1956.

Lee, Marie G. *Finding My Voice.* Houghton Mifflin, 1994.

Nelson, Vaunda Micheaux. *Mayfield Crossing.* Philomel, 1993.

Norton, Mary. *The Borrowers.* Harcourt, 1953.

Oughton, Jerrie. *Music From a Place Called Half Moon.* Houghton, 1995.

Paulsen, Gary. *Harris and Me: A Summer Remembered.* Harcourt, 1993.

Salisbury, Graham. *Blue Skin of the Sea: A Novel in Stories.* Doubleday, 1992.

Smothers, Ethel Footman. *Down in the Piney Woods.* Knopf, 1992.

*Sorenson, Virginia. *Miracles on Maple Hill.* Harcourt, 1957.

*Speare, Elizabeth George. *The Witch of Blackbird Pond.* Houghton, 1959.

Strauch, Eileen Walsh. *Hey You, Sister Rose.* Tambourine, 1993.

White, E. B. *Charlotte's Web.* Harper, 1952.

White, Ruth. *Sweet Creek Holler.* Farrar, 1988.

Wilkinson, Brenda. *Not Separate, Not Equal.* Harper, 1987.

*Yates, Elizabeth. *Amos Fortune, Free Man.* Dutton, 1951.

Nonfiction

Beals, Melba Patillo. *Warriors Don't Cry: A Searing Memoir of the Battle to Integrate Little Rock's Central High School.* Pocket/Archway, 1995.

Davis, Kenneth C. *Don't Know Much About History.* Crown Publishers, Inc., 1990.

Duden, Jane. *Timelines. 1950s.* Crestwood House, 1989.

English, June. *Transportation. Automobiles to Zeppelins.* Scholastic, Inc., 1995.

Hakim, Joy. *All the People.* Oxford University Press, 1995.

Isserman, Maurice. *America at War. The Korean War.* Facts on File, 1992.

Levine, Ellen. *Freedom's Children: Young Civil Rights Activists Tell Their Own Stories.* Putnam, 1993.

Lindop, Edmund. *An Album of the Fifties.* Franklin Watts, 1978.

Rubel, David. *The Scholastic Encyclopedia of the Presidents and Their Times.* Scholastic Inc., 1994.

——*The United States in the 20th Century.* Scholastic Inc., 1995.

Seigel, Beatrice. *The Year They Walked.* Macmillan, 1992.

Sharman, Margaret. *Take Ten Years. 1950s.* Steck-Vaughn Company, 1993.

Smith, Carter, ed. *Presidents in a Time of Change.* The Millbrook Press, 1993.

Wood, Richard, ed. *Great Inventions.* Time-Life Books, 1995.

Teacher Created Materials

#064 *Share the Olympic Dream*

#296 Thematic Unit: *Archaeology*

#477 Learning Through Literature: *Geography*

#494 *Focus on Artists*

#396 *Focus on Inventors*

Answer Key

Page 13
1. < 2. > 3. <
4. < 5. < 6. <
7. > 8. > 9. <
10. < 11. >
12. <

Page 15
1. Juneau
2. Point Barrow
3. Prudhoe
4. Valdez
5. Yukon
6. Alaska Range
7. Mt. McKinley
8. Aleutian
9. Arctic
10. Bering
11. Pacific

Page 16
1. Oahu
2. Molokai
3. Hawaii
4. Kauai
5. Maui
6. Kahoolawe
7. Lanai
8. Niihau

Page 20
1. Mamie
2. Mamie
3. Bess
4. Both
5. Bess
6. Mamie
7. Mamie
8. Bess
9. Mamie
10. Bess
11. Bess
12. Bess
13. Mamie
14. Mamie
15. Bess
16. Mamie
17. both
18. Mamie
19. Bess
20. Bess
21. Mamie
22. Bess
23. Bess
24. Mamie
25. Mamie

Page 22
1. 33,936,234
2. 89
3. 442
4. 27,314,992
5. 26,022,752
6. 457
7. 35,590,472
8. 73
Challenge:
61,251,226;
61,613,224

Page 23
Math: 1. Eisenhower -
83%; Stevenson -
17%
2. 35,590,472
Map: Check for
correct responses; the
following states
should be colored
blue: Arkansas,
Louisiana, Kentucky,
Georgia, Mississippi,
Alabama, South
Carolina, North
Carolina, and West
Virginia

Page 27
(map)
1. China
2. North Korea
3. South Korea
4. USSR
5. Pyongyang
6. Seoul
7. 38th Parallel
8. Sea of Japan
9. Yellow Sea

Page 43
1. clean
2. sparkled
3. project
4. weekly
5. loans
6. layout
7. boulevard
8. exotic
9. disaster
10. asphalt

11. flooded
12. telecast
13. success
14. seven
15. visitor

Page 49 answers may vary

Page 52
All should be circled
except flashlight,
fountain pen, and
blender.

Page 54
1. Mount Vernon
2. childhood
3. scholarships
4. editor-in-chief
5. president
6. writing
7. published
8. children's
9. *Charlotte's Web*
10. adults
11. guidebook
12. Freedom
13. awards
14. Newbery
15. disease

Page 67
1. 65
2. 61
3. 27
4. 24
5. 233
6. 30
7. 35
8. 1.5
9. 45
10. 724

Page 73
1. D
2. H
3. G
4. A
5. B
6. C
7. E
8. F

Page 75
1. China
2. area
3. inhabitants
4. Himalayas
5. Nepal
6. plateau
7. elevation
8. mountains
9. Mt. Everest
10. Po
11. climate
12. temperatures
13. monsoons
14. rain

Page 83

Across
2. pedal pushers
4. rock and roll
5. dungarees
7. television
8. petticoats
9. hand jive
10. TV dinners
11. drive-in
13. coffee house

Down
1. Mad Magazine
3. saddle shoes
6. beatniks
12. pencil
14. Frisbee

Page 84
blue-suede shoes—
Elvis Presley
architect—Frank
Lloyd Wright
red hair—Lucille
Ball
Red Scare—
Joseph McCarthy
The Cat in the Hat—
Dr. Seuss
head of NAACP—
Thurgood Marshall
composer &
conductor—Leonard
Bernstein
Magic Kingdom—
Walt Disney

the Beat
Generation—
Jack Kerouac
accused of
espionage—Julius
and Ethel Rosenberg
polio—Dr. Jonas Salk
seamstress—
Rosa Parks

Page 85
1. 49,983,000
2. 18.5 bilion
3. 103,000
4. 350,000,000
5. 15 miles
6. 4,875,000
7. $60,000
8. 88,116
9. $150,000
10. 504
11. 140 million
12. $39,600,000

Page 86
1. 1957
2. 1951
3. 1959
4. 1952
5. 1953
6. 1956
7. 1950
8. 1952
9. 1955
10. 1957
11. 1958
12. 1954